Valuing Data
An Open Framework

T0338483

Valuing Data

An Open Framework

Dewey E. Ray

CRC Press

Taylor & Francis Group
Boca Raton London New York

CRC Press is an imprint of the
Taylor & Francis Group, an **informa** business

CRC Press
Taylor & Francis Group
6000 Broken Sound Parkway NW, Suite 300
Boca Raton, FL 33487-2742

International Standard Book Number-13: 978-1-1382-9774-6 (Hardback)

Library of Congress Cataloging-in-Publication Data

Names: Ray, Dewey E., author.
Title: Valuing data : an open framework / Dewey E. Ray.
Description: Boca Raton, FL : CRC Press, 2017.
Identifiers: LCCN 2017025819 | ISBN 9781138297746 (hbk : alk. paper)
Subjects: LCSH: Management information systems. | Database management. | Business intelligence. | Business--Data processing. | Information technology--Management.
Classification: LCC HD30.213 .R39 2017 | DDC 658.15--dc23
LC record available at https://lccn.loc.gov/2017025819

Visit the Taylor & Francis Web site at
http://www.taylorandfrancis.com

and the CRC Press Web site at
http://www.crcpress.com

Contents

Introduction

The past couple of decades have seen a dramatic increase in the amount and variety of information that is generated and stored electronically within business enterprises. According to a 2014 study by the International Data Corporation, the volume of digital bits generated across the globe is doubling in size every two years and by the year 2020 will reach 44 zettabytes, or 44 trillion bytes. For the typical business enterprise, this translates into an average annual growth in data of 40%, and as business models continue to evolve toward more technology-enabled variants, this will only increase. Storing the increased volume of information has not been a problem to date, but as these information stores grow larger and larger, multiple challenges arise for senior management, namely, questions such as "How much is our data worth?" "Are we storing our data in the most cost-effective way?" "Are we managing our data effectively and efficiently?" "Do we know which data is most important?" "Are we extracting business insight from the right data?" "Are our data adding to the value of our business?" "Are our data a liability?" "What is the potential for monetizing our data?" and "Do we have an appropriate risk management plan in place to protect our data?"

Instead of pursuing answers to these "value-based" questions, many companies choose to spend millions on new information technology (IT) systems believing that this is the best pathway to value creation through technology. Other companies choose to treat IT as an expense item that should be kept to a minimum, resulting in the relegation of electronically stored information, or data, to the role of mere inputs and outputs in the operational cogs of the business.

Both of these IT strategies may benefit a business in the short run, but both ignore the hidden value within the data. In order to answer these value-based questions, data must be treated with the same rigor and discipline as other tangible and intangible assets. In other words, corporate data should be treated as a potential asset and should have its own asset valuation methodology that is accepted by the business community, the accounting and valuation community, and other important stakeholder groups.

Clearly, there is a need for enterprise tools that will enable management to address the challenges—and questions—that surround the management and valuation of the data asset. This book is a first step in that direction. Its purpose is to

- Provide the reader with some background on the nature of data
- Present the common categories of business data
- Explain the importance of data management
- Report the current thinking on data valuation
- Offer some business reasons to value data
- Present an "open framework"—along with some proposed methods—for valuing data

The book does not aim to prescribe exactly how data should be valued monetarily, but rather to serve as a "starting point" for a discussion of data valuation with the objective of developing a stakeholder consensus, which, in turn, will become accepted standards and practices.

Thank you for your interest and future participation in this process.

Disclaimer

- The framework is not warranted for any particular purpose other than suggested guidance on how to value the data asset.
- The rules that govern the valuation of assets for financial reporting purposes are controlled by the Financial Accounting Standards Board, IASB, generally accepted accounting principles, and other regulatory entities. Nothing in this book is intended to abrogate those rules in any way.
- The author grants all individuals and groups the right to use the content of this book in any way they choose and all users must accept all liability arising from the use of the material contained in the book, holding the author and publisher harmless from any outcome resulting from the usage of this book.
- The phrase "The Open Framework for Data Valuation" is trademarked.

Author

Dewey E. Ray has spent over 35 years in the information technology (IT) field in a variety of technical, consulting, and managerial roles. Beginning as a FORTRAN programmer on IBM and Control Data mainframes, his early IT jobs included designing, programming, and implementing a variety of applications and systems. As the IT field evolved, so did his interests, and in the ensuing years, Mr. Ray became an Internet and enterprise architecture specialist, while leading several IT consulting practices focused on e-business and distributed system architecture design. His position titles have included programmer, systems analyst, systems manager, senior systems engineer, region technical marketing manager, principal consultant, practice director, chief technology officer, chief information officer, and trainer. In addition to his IT roles, his work experience also includes mergers and aquisitions (M&A) buy-side and sell-side IT due diligence and integration.

1

Uncovering the Hidden Asset

The idea that business data has value associated with it is widely acknowledged, but if it does, why is it not included as a separate asset category in a business valuation or reported on corporate balance sheets?

These are the questions that I posed to numerous business, financial, and information technology executives over the past couple of years:

"In your opinion, is business data an asset?"

"If so, should business data be reported on a company's balance sheet?"

"Why isn't business data being reported as an asset?"

The responses were a resounding "yes" to the first two questions and the response to the third question most often was "It's because of accounting rules."

So, I wondered, if the experts agree that data is an asset that should be reported on a company's balance sheet why is this not happening? In other words:

> "Why do accounting rules prevent businesses from reporting the value of their data assets?"

I set out to find the answer to this question and began my investigation by analyzing how current accounting rules control asset reporting. Next, I asked my accountant friends to explain why business data is not treated as an asset. The answer, I discovered, is largely a result of how generally accepted accounting principles (i.e., GAAP) define and value assets.

To understand how business asset valuation works, let's briefly review assets and how they are valued.

What Are Assets and How Are They Valued?

Simply put, assets are things that a company has acquired, that have future economic value, and that can be measured and expressed in dollars. There are two categories of assets—tangible and intangible—and GAAP requires that in order for an item to be treated as an asset, it must have a "fair value" associated with it.

The Fair Value Approach to Asset Valuation

Fair value is the generally accepted standard for valuing business assets for financial reporting purposes (i.e., the balance sheet) and is based on the assumption that the marketplace will determine what a business asset is worth.

Here's how it works.

Let's say two parties meet for the purpose of exchanging money for an item. After discussing the relevant facts surrounding the item, taking into account the advantages and disadvantages that each will gain from the sale of the item, the parties agree on a price and complete the transaction. The completion of the transaction, in turn, establishes a historical price or cost for the item—depending on whether the party is a seller (i.e., selling price) or buyer (i.e., cost of acquisition). Further, assume that similar items are being bought and sold on a regular basis, providing a public history of prices paid for this particular item. With this history of similar transactions publicly available, along with the prices paid, the fair market value of the item can now be reliably determined by buyers, sellers, accountants, valuation experts, and other interested parties.

Next, let's look at how the two basic categories of assets are valued.

Valuing Tangible Assets

Tangible assets are physical things such as property, plant, equipment, and inventory. For example, when a business produces a product, it typically applies raw materials, labor, and processes to the production task. The output from the production task is then sold, and in the process, a historical price (or cost) is established upon which to base a fair value. As a result of this process, calculating the fair value of the company's product inventory becomes fairly straightforward: Simply multiply the price of each item sold by the number of equivalent units within the inventory.

Valuing Intangible Assets

Intangible assets are nonphysical things that provide value or a marketplace advantage and are deemed to have a useful life of more than one year. They typically consist of intellectual property items such as copyrights, trademarks, and licensing agreements. Based upon the GAAP guidelines, intangible assets can only be valued for financial reporting purposes if they were acquired, have an identifiable value, and can be amortized. For example, a company logo that was developed internally will not appear on the company balance sheet as an intangible asset because it has no acquisition price or cost associated with it, even though it may have huge name recognition value. On the other hand, patents that have been purchased or acquired from another party can be included on the balance sheet if they meet the other GAAP requirements.

The Nature of Data Assets

So, is business data a tangible or intangible asset and, if it is an asset, is the fair value approach to asset valuation applicable? To answer this question, I analyzed the nature of data from a GAAP perspective and here's what I discovered.

First, since data is typically stored in a digital or electronic form, it is nonphysical and, therefore, intangible. Business data generally meets this GAAP requirement.

Second, to qualify as an intangible asset on the balance sheet, the asset must have identifiable value, have a determinate life, and be amortizable. Business data meets these GAAP requirements *if* the data has an acquisition price or cost associated with it. However, business data that is generated internally—as most business data is—typically does not have a fair value price/cost associated with it, and thus, it does not meet this GAAP requirement.

Therefore, like the company logo that was created in-house, internally generated business data cannot appear on financial reports as a unique or separate asset category. As a result, the true value of a firm's data assets is hidden from public view!

Voila! I finally had my answer.

How Is Business Data Valued?

Valuation experts have long known that business data can represent significant value, especially in Internet-based business models. Companies such as Amazon, Facebook, and Google are obvious examples, but as more traditional businesses have expanded their use of information technology, the increased role of data has, in many companies, added significantly to the overall value of the businesses.

For example, valuation analysts and business investors often evaluate a firm's data in terms of how the data can be monetized or synergized with the goal of increasing revenue or value. Monetization involves packaging the data in a way that allows it to be sold by the owners. Synergizing data involves integrating the data of two businesses—typically as the result of a merger or acquisition—in ways that result in a combined value that exceeds the sum of the individual firms' data. These informal, "off-balance sheet" valuations of data assets can significantly impact the perceived value of a business and the resulting offer price from potential acquirers or private equity investors.

Another way business data is valued is through use of the "Goodwill" category of intangible assets.

The best example of a goodwill asset is the reputation of the firm in its marketplace and the impact its reputation has upon the perceived value of its business. Since goodwill has no identifiable assets associated with it, strictly speaking, it does not exist until a business is purchased by another firm. For example, if a target firm's total net asset value is $12 and a buyer pays $20 for the business, the difference of $8 is considered goodwill.

In business valuations, goodwill is sometimes expanded to include that portion of a firm's value that cannot be attributed to any other income producing assets—tangible or intangible. For example, a privately held firm may feel that the high quality and abundance of its data justifies a higher valuation and, lacking a "GAAP-approved" category for their data assets, will attribute the higher valuation to goodwill. Since goodwill has no predetermined value until a firm is acquired, the inclusion of the data asset isn't breaking the accounting rules—perhaps just bending them a bit. For a publicly held firm, the market is constantly valuing its business up or down anyway, so goodwill is always being evaluated regardless of its composition.

To summarize, the value of business data is routinely acknowledged through off-balance sheet valuation activities and its inclusion in goodwill, but these acknowledgments often mask the true value of the asset.

Business data truly is a hidden asset!

Can Business Data Also Be a Liability?

So, if business data is a hidden asset, can it also be a hidden liability? Most definitely! We don't typically think of internally generated business data as representing a liability; however, the increasingly vital role that data plays in a variety of industries and business models as an asset also creates situations in which it can pose a liability. In fact, as important as it may be to determine the value of data, it is equally important to understand the business liability that can accrue to business data.

What do I mean by liability? Accounting rules define liability as "obligations of the company" or as "a claim against a company's assets." A company's balance sheet will typically list several liability accounts, most ending with the word "payable," all representing commitments that the company has made.

The question then is "how does business data fit into the traditional accounting rules as a potential liability?" One would not expect a firm's internally generated data to appear as a liability on the balance sheet, especially as a "payable." So, if business data represents a potential liability, what kind of liability are we talking about? To answer this question, let's take a look at some conditions that might infuse business data with liability.

Unauthorized Disclosure of Data

Businesses have a fiduciary responsibility to protect personal data, such as customer information, from unauthorized disclosure. In fact, many financial institutions implement contractual obligations among themselves and their trading partners that hold the trading partners liable if customer financial data, such as credit card information, is stolen or disclosed in an unauthorized fashion. Firms that have had their data stolen are acutely aware of the financial liability that can be associated with data.

Inadequate Compliance Data

Many industries are required to maintain extensive records documenting their compliance with applicable laws and regulations. If the data is inadequately or improperly maintained, and as a result, exposes the company to violations of the law or regulations, then a potential liability is created. Firms that have been audited by a regulatory agency and found to be in violation of applicable laws or regulations are very knowledgeable of the fines that can be imposed as a result of violations.

Flawed Data Used in Analytics

Good business analytics is predicated upon the assumption that the data that is being used is of high value—meaning that it is, among other things, of high quality. If the input data for analytics is flawed or of low quality, then the resulting analytics may also be flawed—to the extent that business decisions based upon the analytics are erroneous. Erroneous conclusions that lead to poor business decisions can cause management to introduce business liabilities that could have been avoided—liabilities that could ultimately threaten the firm's financial survival.

Monetized Data

As more businesses seek ways to package and sell their data, they want to make sure that the data being sold is of high quality and high value. As with other business products, a data product that fails to deliver value can be perceived as a liability if the customer finds flaws or errors in the data.

Clearly, business data does not fit the traditional definition of a liability such as one would see on a balance sheet, but it can represent a liability nonetheless. It's unlikely that management would consider purchasing cyber insurance to protect the business in the event their customer data is stolen if they did not believe that their data represent a potential liability!

Is My Business Data an Asset or a Liability?

The answer to this question for most businesses is "it's a mixed bag"; that is, some of their data has real value and is obviously an asset, while other data—for a variety of reasons—represents a real liability to the firm. As a business leader, you may be asking:

> *If my business data is an asset, what is its value and how can I leverage this value; and if some of my business data is also a liability, why is this and what can I do to turn it into an asset?*

The remaining chapters of this book will help you determine the answer to this question.

How to Proceed with This Book

This book was written for a broad audience that includes business, accounting, and technology professionals. Depending upon your area of interest, you may want to focus on only some of the remaining chapters. Here are my recommendations on how to proceed:

If you are primarily a business leader, I suggest that you scan Chapters 2–4 to get a high-level understanding of what data is, how it should be managed, and the basic categories of business data. Then I recommend a thorough read of Chapters 5 and 6 to gain insight into what other thought leaders are saying about valuing data and how valuing data can potentially help your business.

If you are an accounting, data, or IT professional, I recommend a thorough read of Chapters 2–4 and a scan of Chapters 5–6. Chapter 7 will be of interest if you plan to participate in actual data valuations.

If you are a business valuation professional interested in the topic of data valuation, I recommend that you read the entire book.

2
AN OVERVIEW OF DATA

What Is Data?

When I launched the data valuation project, my first task was to define what data is. Embracing the axiom "you can't value something unless you can measure it, and you can't measure something unless you can define it," I sought out a definition that was sufficiently broad yet concise enough to serve as the foundation for an open framework for data valuation.

As I evaluated various definitions, I found agreement on the following points: Data is a form of information, is typically stored on a computer, and is essential to the running of a business—or organization. However, beyond this general description, opinions diverge. This is because the term is used in many different contexts and connotations; thus, its meaning is often defined by the context in which it is used. Knowing that a narrow, contextual definition would not be suitable, I decided to take a "top–down" look at the origins of the term and how it is used.

Digital Assets

When I looked at how the industry has defined data, the term "digital assets" emerged as a high-level categorization. Simply put, digital assets is a catch-all category for electronic artifacts, or files, including images, multimedia, text, data, and pretty much everything else produced by a digital device. The definition does make one important distinction: A digital artifact, or file, is not considered an "asset" unless it has descriptive information, such as metadata, associated with it. I think this distinction is significant because it excludes things like operating system files, temporary files, and other transient information that may exist at one time or another on a firm's computer system but whose existence is transitory or of a special-use nature.

So, my initial finding regarding the definition of data is that in order for it to be considered a digital asset, it should have some amount of metadata associated with it.

Digital Assets vs. Data Assets

The next step in my quest to define data involved examining the differences between data that is considered a digital asset—that is, it has descriptive metadata associated with it—and the other categories of digital assets. To help with this differentiation, I looked at some common industry definitions of data.

Here is what I found.

Some Definitions of "Data"

Merriam-Webster defines data as "factual information (as measurements or statistics) used as a basis for reasoning, discussion, or calculation."

Business Dictionary.com expands on the Merriam-Webster definition by defining data as "information in raw or organized form (such as alphabets, numbers, or symbols) that refer to, or represent conditions, ideas, or objects."

The Data Management Association defines the term more broadly as "the representation of facts as text, numbers, graphics, images, sound or video."

The information technology field typically defines data as "the quantities, characters, or symbols on which operations are performed by a computer, being stored and transmitted in the form of electrical signals and recorded on magnetic, optical, or mechanical recording media."

Each of these definitions offers a useful perspective on the nature of data, but none of them provide the foundational definition needed to establish a measurement system for data valuation. This prompted me to formulate a definition for data suitable for the Open Framework for Data Valuation™.

The Open Framework Definition of Data

For the purpose of the Open Framework for Data Valuation, data is defined as follows:

> Information, facts, and statistics represented as numbers or text that are collected for reference, observation, measurement, and analysis; have metadata associated with it; are stored on electronic media (e.g. magnetic, optical), and are capable of being transmitted in the form of electrical signals.

In other words, this definition assumes that "data" is captured and stored inside a computer system and thus is available for retrieval, examination, manipulation, and processing. In the interest of grammatical correctness, data is the plural of *datum*, a single piece of information. However, it is a common practice to use *data* as both the singular and plural form of the word; thus, we will adhere to the common usage throughout this book.

Nondata Digital Assets

We now have a definition of "data," but what about the digital assets that *are not* data and how do they fit into our framework for valuing data? The answer: They don't and that's because the Open Framework for Data Valuation is about "data" and data alone. I recognize that nondata digital assets are important to the business and many have significant value, but they are excluded, by design, from the scope of this book.

Figure 2.1 depicts examples of the digital assets of a typical enterprise.

Structured Data—An Overview

Based upon the Open Framework for Data Valuation definition, data can be further categorized as structured or unstructured. Structured data is defined as follows:

> Data that is stored in a consistent electronic form and format which, as a result, allows it to be accessed, interpreted, and prepared for subsequent use (i.e. retrieval, examination, manipulation, and processing).

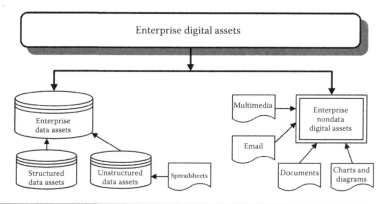

Figure 2.1 Enterprise digital assets.

Storing data in a consistent form and format implies that a software application was created for the purpose of capturing and storing the data and that the stored data will produce reliable results each time it is accessed and interpreted. This is an important concept because structured data derives much of its value as an asset from the fact that *it is* structured.

Some Data Management Terms and Definitions

Throughout this book, certain industry-standard terms will be used when referring to data, how it is stored, and how it is managed. Table 2.1 presents these terms, along with their definitions.

Common Methods for Storing and Managing Structured Data

How data is stored can impact the potential value of the asset based upon the ease of use, structural integrity, and flexibility of the storage method. The following overview provides a basis for evaluating the strengths and weaknesses of the common methods for storing data in a structured format. Here's a description of each.

Flat Data File Format

The term "flat data file" is generally used to describe a data file format in which data elements or items are stored sequentially as alphanumeric characters with a special character used for delineating or separating the individual elements or items from each other. This is

Table 2.1 Some Data Terms and Definitions

TERM	DEFINITION
Data file	Data that is stored in an electronic file (e.g., on tape, disk, USB, etc.), typically in a format that can be interpreted.
Sequential data file	A data file containing multiple instances of individual data elements that can be accessed and read electronically (by an appropriate application software tool) in a sequential fashion. This format assumes a form of sequential consistency throughout the data file.
Index	Unique "keys" that point to other information, typically individual records containing data that is contained within the database. Indexes may be combined with a sequential data file to create an indexed-sequential data file. Relational databases also make extensive use of indexing techniques.
Data model	A set of data specifications and related diagrams that reflect the data requirements and designs associated with a particular database. There are two forms of the data model: A Logical Model and a Physical Model. The Logical Model describes the master data entities, the operational data entities, and transactional data entities and their relationships. The Physical Model is normally embedded within the actual structure of the relational database in the form of database tables and keys.
Database	An organized collection of related data objects, elements, or entities with built-in functional support for updating, manipulating, processing, and retrieving the contents of the database.
Table	A set of rows and columns in a relational database.
Row	A relational data set representing a single instance of an item or entity type. For example, within a table named "Customer," one might see multiple rows in the table with labels such as "Customer Name," "Customer Address," and "Customer Gender."
Column	A relational data element that contains attributes associated with the rows in a table. For example, the first column in a table named "Customer" would likely contain data associated with Customer A, and the next column would likely contain data associated with Customer B, and so forth.
Entity	A data object that can be uniquely identified based upon its name and its attributes. Entities can be expressed as nouns, for example, Customer, Employee, and Product. In relational database terminology, a table containing rows and columns of related data would be called an "entity."
Attribute	A specification that defines the properties or nature of a data object. For example, a data object or entity with the name "Customer" would likely have attributes such as Customer Name, Customer Address, and Customer Gender associated with it.
Data element	A field, column, row, or attribute that describes some data object within a database. It will have a name, a definition, and a meaning. A collection of data elements form a data structure.
Metadata	Information that describes the physical data stored in databases. It includes descriptions of the logical and physical database structures, data elements, associated business processes, application systems, and business rules.

sometimes referred to as delimited text file and is often used as a format for exporting/importing data from one storage system (i.e., application or database) to another.

While a flat data file is, technically speaking, a structured form of data storage, its simple structure does not add as much value to the data as do the more sophisticated data storage structures.

Indexed-Sequential Data File Format

The Indexed-Sequential Data File format adds an important feature to the flat data file through the use of an index or key. Often referred to as the Indexed Sequential Access Method (ISAM), the index enables individual data elements to be easily retrieved, examined, manipulated, and processed. For example, an index might be a customer identification number which, when entered into the data management system, retrieves the customer record containing all of the information associated with that particular customer.

Indexed-Sequential Data File structures are very limited in terms of flexibility but are a significant improvement over the flat data file format. Developed during the early years of information technology evolution, most have been upgraded to more structured data storage and management systems. Some examples are Berkeley DB, Btrieve, Dbase, Clipper, Foxpro, Microsoft Access, and Paradox.

Hierarchical Database Model

The hierarchical model is based upon a parent–child relationship between data elements or items that link the data elements to each other in a hierarchical or inverted tree fashion. This model makes it fairly easy to search and retrieve individual data elements, but the user must know the stored value of the "parent" data element in order to access its subordinate data elements. While the hierarchical model offers much more sophisticated data storage and management capabilities than the indexed-sequential data file format, it adds very little value to the data from a management perspective. The IBM Information Management System (IMS) is an example of a hierarchical database system.

Network Database Model

The network database model data is organized into "sets" that contain the individual data elements or items related to the set and the different sets are linked to each other via a common owner record. The structure appears on the surface to be simple but can become very complex as a database grows in size—making maintenance and updating very difficult. In addition, retrieving data from this model requires that the user have an intimate understanding of the data sets within the network and their contents. The CA Technologies CA-Integrated Database Management System (CA-IDMS) is the best known example of a networked database management system.

Neither the hierarchical model nor network models support high-level ad hoc queries, thus requiring that complex software applications be written to retrieve and manipulate the data. As a result of these weaknesses, most business organizations began phasing out the hierarchical and network models in the 1990s, but some remain in service today.

Relational Database Model

The relational database model was developed in the 1980s as a solution to the weaknesses of the hierarchical and network database models and over the past 30 years has evolved into the industry standard model for storing and managing corporate data assets.

The underlying structure in a relational database model is based upon the concept of "tables" containing "rows" and "columns" of data. Tables are given names such as "Customer Table" and "Product Table," and each row within the table represents a unique element or item. For example, a row in a relational table might be labeled "Customer Name," and all of the data fields appearing in the corresponding columns would contain unique instances of actual customer names. The relational database model is very flexible, and retrieval of the data is quite easy and straightforward. In addition, designating a data field (e.g., Customer Name) as a key makes it possible for searches to be performed quickly and efficiently across both multiple tables and data fields. Some of the benefits of the relational database model are the following:

- Easy to understand and use—from an end-user perspective
- External applications can be easily interfaced with a relational database
- Modifying and updating the database are relatively easy
- Referential integrity

Among the better known relational database model software products are Oracle's RDBMS, Microsoft's SQL Server, IBM's DB2, SQL Anywhere, PostgreSQL, MySQL, Ingres, Teradata, Informix, and Hadoop.

Artificial Intelligence

Artificial intelligence (AI) offers the potential to revolutionize several areas within the information technology field and data is one of those. Strictly speaking, AI is not a new data storage structure and management technology in and of itself, but rather a technology layer that can be integrated with traditional database technologies to enhance the utilization of existing data stores. Some of the areas in which AI and database management can be utilized are the following:

- Predictive analytics in which algorithms are able to suggest future uses for existing data based upon current usage.
- Machine learning algorithms that can speed up the data preparation process, trigger actions based upon the type of data, and analyze temporal factors to prevent potential financial fraud.
- Integrating structured data with unstructured data to provide improved analytics. This includes the ability to contextualize enormous quantities of data from disparate sources resulting in deep learning that predicts patterns and accelerates the analytical process.
- Advanced pattern recognition, particularly as it relates to voice, image, and visual data.

These evolutionary developments in AI database integration are producing systems that are capable of advanced knowledge processing,

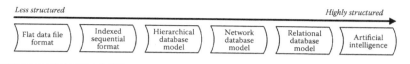

Figure 2.2　Unstructured to structured data continuum.

resulting in significant enhancements to the value of large corporate databases using this technology.

Figure 2.2 depicts a progressive continuum across which a set of data may evolve from a relatively unstructured format to a highly structured format.

Unstructured Data—An Overview

In contrast to structured data, *unstructured data* can be defined as follows:

> Data that is stored in a form and format which prevents electronic access for the purpose of *direct* retrieval, examination, manipulation, or processing.

A key term in the definition of unstructured data that distinguishes it from structured data is the word *direct*—which means "without having to perform intermediate preparation steps," such as keying the data into another software application, scanning and digitizing the data, or having to export/import—all activities that might be required to move data from an unstructured format into a structured format.

The unstructured data definition includes data that is stored in other digital assets (e.g., a blog, document, image, video, spreadsheet, etc.) or in nonelectronic information assets, such as hard-copy books and printed documents.

Unstructured data often has significant business value; however, the cost of extracting and transferring the data (e.g., from a spreadsheet to a relational database table) can adversely impact its value, making it more difficult to methodically and reliably calculate the business value of the data while in an unstructured state.

For these reasons, I have chosen to treat unstructured data as a potential digital asset rather than a data asset.

Summary

There are a lot of perspectives on "what data is," and understanding the nature of this asset is essential to the development of a reliable and repeatable methodology for valuing it. Based upon my research findings and the purpose of the Open Framework for Data Valuation, I propose the following basic definition of data:

> Information, facts, and statistics represented as numbers or text that are collected for reference, observation, measurement, and analysis; are stored on electronic media (e.g., magnetic, optical); and are capable of being transmitted in the form of electrical signals.

But in order to develop a method for valuing data in a reliable and repeatable manner, I believe that data—as defined previously—must also be stored in a structured format. This compels me to add the following requirement to the basic definition:

> Data that is stored in a consistent electronic form and format which, as a result, allows it to be accessed, interpreted, and prepared for subsequent use (i.e., retrieval, examination, manipulation, and processing).

In summary, combining the basic definition of data with the requirement that the data also be stored in a structured format has resulted in the following definition:

> Information, facts, and statistics represented as numbers or text that are collected for reference, observation, measurement, and analysis; are stored in a consistent format on electronic media; and are capable of being accessed, interpreted, and prepared for subsequent use (i.e., retrieval, examination, manipulation, processing, and transmittal).

For the purposes of The Open Framework for Data Valuation, this definition will be used throughout the book.

3

THE COMMON CATEGORIES OF BUSINESS DATA

Depending upon their business model and how they choose to categorize their data, a business enterprise may have several categories of data stored within their information systems. That being said, most businesses have at least the following three basic categories of data:

- *Transactional Data* that supports the daily operations of the enterprise
- *Analytical Data* that supports enterprise analysis and decision-making
- *Master Data* that represents the key entities upon which transactions are executed and the dimensions around which analysis is conducted

Figure 3.1 depicts the three basic categories of business data.
An overview of each of the basic categories follows.

Transactional Data

Transactional data is generated and updated within the firm's operational systems as the business executes its processes throughout its supply or service chain. In other words, transactional data describes an action or event within the business and has a time dimension associated with it. These business processes typically include the following:

- Product and service sales
- Order management
- Purchasing and accounts payable
- Manufacturing or service delivery
- Shipping and billing
- Accounts receivable and payment collection

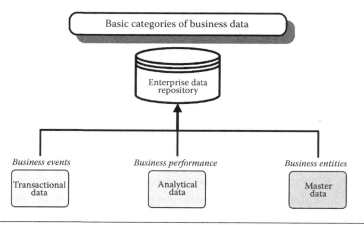

Figure 3.1   Basic categories of business data.

Table 3.1   Examples of Transactional Data

Customer name	Invoice number	Order/invoice total amount
Customer address	Order date/time	Discount amount
Supplier name	Product model number	Shipping costs
Supplier address	Order quantity	Net amount of order/invoice
Customer order number	Unit price	Payment method

Table 3.1 contains examples of transactional data that is generated during the execution of the firm's business processes.

Transactional data is generally processed through online processing systems, and as the transactions are processed, the data is stored in relational database tables. Because of the time dimension associated with it, some of the transactional data may become less relevant and potentially less valuable over time.

Analytical Data

Analytical data is numerical data that has been extracted from transaction database tables, along with other sources, and stored in online analytical processing repositories—such as data warehouses and data marts. Using business analytics software, analytical data can be loaded into multidimensional arrays for the purpose of analyzing relationships between the disparate data elements. This is the basis for

Table 3.2   Examples of Analytical Data

Customer name	Order/invoice total amount	Order date/time
Product model number	Discount amount	Ship to location
Number of units ordered	Net amount of order/invoice	Unit production date
Unit price	Payment method	Unit production cost

discovering business insights that can be monetized or exploited in some way.

Table 3.2 contains some examples of data that might be extracted for the purpose of analysis.

Master Data

Master data is defined as "data about the business data entities that provide context for business transactions." In other words, a firm's master data describes persons, places, or things, such as customers, products, employees, inventory, and suppliers, around which business transactions are executed. Master data is typically static, nontransactional data utilized by multiple systems and is the most accurate and definitive data that exists within the organization. Master data values are considered the "golden data asset" within the enterprise, and their existence is highly protected—or should be.

A firm's Master Database is often integrated with its Reference Database (also known as the Data Dictionary), and together, the two databases provide a definitive source of reference throughout the business. Table 3.3 contains some examples of data that might appear in the enterprise Master Database.

Some Functional Categories of Business Data

In addition to the three basic categories, business data can also be categorized based upon its functional role within the organization.

Table 3.3   Examples of Master Data

Customer name	Product model number	Unit production date
Customer address	Order number	Production location
Supplier name	Product description	Invoice number
Supplier address	Unit price	Payment method

Here are some basic functions which involve data in a supporting role:

- Finance
- Operations
- Compliance
- Strategic planning
- Research and development

The following is an overview of these functional categories of business data.

Financial Data

Financial data refers to those data elements, attributes, and entities that describe the financial history, current financial health, and economic health of the business. Included in this category is data related to the following:

- Chart of accounts
- General ledger
- Account groups (e.g., assets, liabilities, and equity)
- Financial transactions
- Parties in transaction
- Accounts receivable and payable

Operations Data

Operations data refers to those data elements, attributes, and entities that describe the operational aspects of the business. It derives its primary value from supporting the business processes, which in turn enable the business to fulfill its mission and generate revenue. Included in this category is data related to the following:

- Supply or service chain (e.g., production, transactions, inventory, service delivery)
- Accounting data (e.g., customers)
- Resource data (e.g., labor, raw materials)
- Competitor data (e.g., competing companies, products, or services)
- Market data (e.g., customer profiles)

Compliance Data

Compliance data refers to all data belonging or pertaining to the business that is used for the purpose of implementing, validating, or maintaining compliance with laws, rules, regulations, or contracts. Its value lies in its relevance for the purpose of establishing and validating consistency or compliance in a court of law, thus reducing liability and risk to the business. The scope and subcategories of compliance data vary depending upon the business model and location of the business but may include data associated with the following:

- Sarbanes-Oxley
- Payment Card Industry Data Security Standard
- Gramm-Leach-Bliley Act
- ISO/IEC 27001
- Health Insurance Portability and Accountability Act
- General Data Protection Regulation
- Contracts and Schedules (internal compliance)
- Audit Data (e.g., results from various audits, including financial, IT, etc.)

Strategic Planning Data

Strategic planning data refers to data that is captured or acquired for the purpose of helping the business determine strategic direction and set strategic goals. Its value lies in helping business leaders stay up-to-date on trends that may help them plan new products or services and more effective marketing campaigns. These benefits may, in turn, translate into enhanced competitiveness, increased revenue, and improved profitability. Strategic planning data may include the following:

- Economic data (e.g., state of the economies and trends)
- Social statistical data (e.g., demographic social trends, trends in the use of social media)
- Best practices data (e.g., industry-specific practices and standards data)
- Environmental data (e.g., ecological trends that impact products and technologies)
- Labor statistical data (e.g., trends in employee work attitudes and demographics)

- Political data (e.g., political trends that may impact emerging markets)
- Technology data (e.g., technology advances or trends that may impact products and markets)

Research and Development Data

Research and development data refers to data that is created, collected, or acquired for the purpose of producing original research results—typically in the area of new product development. Its primary value lies in the business insights gained as a result of the research, which may, in turn, impact decisions to pursue/not pursue new products, services, or markets. Additional value is derived from ownership of the intellectual property rights associated with the research and development activities, particularly if the business decides to monetize its intellectual property. Research and development data may include the following:

- Laboratory data (e.g., observational, experimental, simulation, derived, and reference)
- Field research data (e.g., data derived from questionnaires, surveys, tests, models, etc.)
- Intellectual property data (e.g., copyright data, patent data, trademark data)

Summary

Business data can be categorized in two ways: By one or more of the three basic categories and/or by its functional category. The three basic categories are

- Transactional
- Analytical
- Master

The functional categories are

- Finance
- Operations
- Compliance

- Strategic Planning
- Research and Development

In terms of assessing the value of a unit of data within the enterprise, one should consider the importance of its role from the perspective of how it is used, how often it is used, and its unique contribution to the firm's business goals and objectives.

4

TAKING A VALUE-
BASED APPROACH TO
DATA MANAGEMENT

Why Is Data Management Important?

Devoting an entire chapter of a book on data valuation to the topic of "data management" strongly suggests that how a business or organization manages its data is important from a valuation perspective—but why? The answer is simple: Data that is subjected to a rigorous data management regimen will likely be of higher quality, more accessible, and more reliable and the descriptive information or metadata will provide useful insights into the nature of the data. Collectively, these characteristics enhance the potential value of data in numerous ways, which will be explained throughout this chapter.

What Is Data Management?

The goal of data management is to

- Understand the data needs of the enterprise
- Capture, store, protect, and preserve the integrity of the data assets
- Improve the quality of data over time
- Prevent unauthorized or inappropriate use of the data
- Provide the tools needed to effectively use the data

The Data Management Association's "Data Management Body of Knowledge" has defined the process of data management in terms of several key functions, nine of which are summarized in Table 4.1.

Each of the nine data management functions contributes to a robust data asset, and each is important to consider when performing a data valuation. Figure 4.1 depicts a hierarchy of the ten data management

27

Table 4.1   Key Data Management Functions

DATA MANAGEMENT FUNCTION	FUNCTION DEFINITION
1. Data governance	Entails exercising authority and control over management of the organization's data assets.
2. Data architecture management	Involves defining the data needs of the enterprise and designing blueprints to meet these needs. This function includes the development and maintenance of enterprise data architecture within the context of the applications and projects that comprise its enterprise architecture.
3. Data development	Involves designing, implementing, and maintaining solutions that meet the data needs of the enterprise. These activities include data modeling, data requirements analysis, the design implementation, and maintenance of data-related system components.
4. Data operations management	Involves the planning, control, and support for the structured data assets across the data life cycle—from creation and acquisition through archival and purge.
5. Metadata management	Involves the planning, implementation, and controls that enable easy access to high quality, integrated metadata.
6. Reference and master data management	Entails planning, implementing, and controlling the data management activities to ensure that a "definitive version" of the contextual data values exists.
7. Data warehousing and business analytics/ intelligence management	Involves planning, implementing, and controlling processes that provide decision support data for knowledge workers engaged in reporting, query, and analysis.
8. Data quality management	Involves the planning, implementation, and control of activities that support quality management techniques that measure, assess, improve, and ensure the fitness of data for use.
9. Data security management	Involves the planning, development, and execution of security policies and procedures for the authentication, authorization, access, and auditing of data and information.

Source: "The DAMA Guide to the Data Management Body of Knowledge." (DAMA-DMBOK) 2009 Data Management Association International, Technics Publications, LLC.

activities, with data governance as the overarching and most important component.

Data Governance

Effective enterprise data management begins with data governance, which embraces the following important goals:

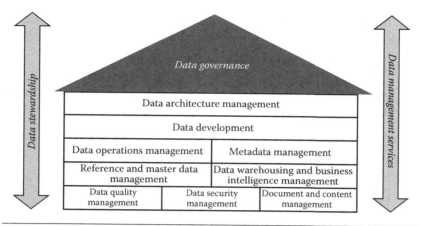

Figure 4.1   The DAMA data management hierarchy. (Note: Since Document & Content Management is not directly related to data, as defined in the book, this function will not be discussed.) (Adapted from "The DAMA Guide to the Data Management Body of Knowledge." (DAMA-DMBOK) 2009 Data Management Association International, Technics Publications, LLC.)

1. Define, approve, and communicate the data management roles, strategy, policies, architecture, procedures, and metrics that have been defined by the enterprise
2. Track and enforce compliance with regulations, policies, standards, architecture, and procedures
3. Sponsor, track, and oversee the delivery of data management projects and services
4. Manage and resolve enterprise-level data-related issues
5. Understand and promote the value of data assets

Data governance is important to the valuation of data because without it, stewardship over this valuable asset could devolve into an informal, ad hoc process, resulting in a decline in data quality. In fact, one of the most important roles in the enterprise is that of "business data steward," who is expected to represent the stakeholders throughout the enterprise while working closely with the information technology (IT) professionals responsible for delivering the technology and tools required to support the data assets. Each enterprise will implement data governance somewhat differently, taking into account the size of the firm and its business strategy, goals, organizational structure, and cultural environment. However, effective data governance programs also have some things in common, namely, a formal structure with defined *roles, strategy, policies, architecture,* and *data standards and procedures.*

Let's take a brief look at each of these.

Data Management Roles

In order to adequately develop and govern the data assets of a large enterprise, several roles need to be defined and staffed by competent individuals. These roles include the following:

- Chief data steward/data officer
- Business data stewards/subject matter experts
- Chief information officer
- Data management executive
- Data analysts
- Database administrators
- Business intelligence specialists

In addition to the data governance roles, larger enterprises may also create steering committees or councils to provide overall direction and guidance to the governance process. Smaller firms may be able to adequately govern their data assets with a subset of the roles found in larger enterprises, but both business and technology roles should exist, along with well-defined role responsibilities for each one.

Data Strategy

A data strategy is a plan for maintaining and improving the quality, integrity, security, and access of the enterprise data. It typically includes business plans that describe how the data will be used to support the enterprise business strategy and goals.

Data Management Policies

Data management policies provide overall guidance for several important data governance areas, including the following:

- Responsibilities of the various business and technology data governance roles

- Expectations regarding the importance of achieving the desired level of quality
- Selection, development, and use of data architecture(s)
- Utilization of data modeling and development of life cycle activities
- Data security, intellectual property, privacy, access, and usage policies
- Data recovery and retention policies

Data management policies can vary greatly from one enterprise to another, but all have one thing in common: They communicate "what to do" and "what not to do" regarding the firm's data assets.

Data Standards and Procedures

Developing, publishing, and adhering to data standards and procedures throughout an enterprise are among the most important data governance functions. Standards are typically developed by data management professionals, then reviewed and adopted by the appropriate council or steering committee.

In addition to standards, the enterprise should also develop written procedures that document the methods, techniques, and steps that are to be followed by the data management professionals. Some of the items that should be addressed in the data standards and procedures guidelines are the following:

- Data modeling and architecture standards
- Business and technical metadata to be captured and maintained
- Data classification standards and procedures
- Standards for database recovery, business continuity, performance, retention, and data acquisition
- Security standards and procedures
- Data cleansing standards and procedures
- Business intelligence standards and procedures

Regulatory Compliance

Increasingly, businesses are finding themselves subjected to a variety of regulations from both the government and industry. In order to comply with these regulations, firms have been compelled to implement capabilities that support the capture and retention of data related to these requirements. Some of the more significant regulatory requirements are the following:

- Sarbanes-Oxley Act of 2002, which imposed stringent new rules for financial accounting and reporting by public companies
- The Health Information Protection and Portability Act, which requires companies to respect the privacy and security of health care information
- The Basel II New Accord and Solvency II from the European Union, which require financial and insurance companies to report certain information regarding their liquidity status
- The Government Accounting Standards and the Financial Accounting Standards Board accounting standards, which define how companies are to manage information assets

Data Architecture Management

Data architecture management has four important objectives:

- Provide a standard business vocabulary for the enterprise data assets
- Describe the boundaries of the enterprise data requirements
- Define the high-level design for integration of all data assets
- Ensure that the enterprise data strategy is fully aligned with the business architecture

Data architecture management is important to the value of data because it helps ensure that the enterprise has defined and stored their data assets in a thoughtful and purposeful way and, in the process, have enhanced the integrity of the individual data elements.

The most significant component of data architecture management is an enterprise data model.

The Enterprise Data Model

The enterprise data model is comprised of several layers that define the business vocabulary of the enterprise and how it conducts its business. Typically produced with a data modeling tool, the artifacts that describe these layers are placed in a central repository where they are protected from unauthorized alteration. Figure 4.2 depicts the layers of an enterprise data model.

The following overview describes the individual layers of a typical enterprise data model.

The Subject Area Model   The subject area model is the highest layer in the enterprise data model and provides the overall "scope" for the enterprise data model. Typically, the subject area layer will be comprised of 10–20 business subjects that describe the enterprise business model.

The Conceptual Data Model   The second layer of the enterprise data model is the conceptual layer or data model. The conceptual data model is important to the enterprise data model because it further defines the business entities and the relationships between the business entities.

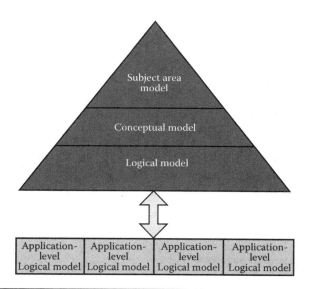

Figure 4.2   Enterprise data model layers. (From "The DAMA Guide to the Data Management Body of Knowledge." (DAMA-DMBOK) 2009 Data Management Association International, Technics Publications, LLC.)

The Logical Data Model   The third layer of the enterprise data model is the logical data model layer. A logical data model, also referred to as an entity relationship model or diagram, describes the data attributes for each entity. The logical data model typically consists of one or more diagrams that depict the essential data attributes for each of the enterprise business entities.

The Application-Level Logical Data Model(s)   Application-level data models are data models that are related to specific applications and are subsets derived from the enterprise data model.

Data Development

Data development is a comprehensive process that resembles, in many ways, the software development life cycle process. It includes the analysis, design, implementation and deployment, and maintenance of data solutions, along with the components needed to support those solutions.

The primary deliverables from the data development process are databases, but also include the following:

- Data requirements documentation
- Business rules surrounding the data requirements
- Data models
- Metadata descriptions/definitions
- Data modeling standards
- Data access and integration services

From a data valuation perspective, the presence of a robust data development program within the enterprise strongly suggests that a disciplined approach has been followed during the development of the firm's data assets, enhancing the potential value of the data asset.

Data Operations Management

Data operations management covers two key areas of data management: database support and technology support. Here's a brief overview of both.

Database Support

Database support is a critical element in data management because it ensures that the data asset is maintained and protected throughout the enterprise. Database support includes

- Creating and maintaining a database production environment, including instances of the database(s)
- Ensuring the performance and integrity of the database(s)
- Implementing procedures for the implementation and changes to the database(s)
- Implementing and executing backup and recovery procedures
- Implementing procedures to provide automatic redundancy and failover
- Implementing procedures to automate the archival of data

Data Technology Support

Data technology support is the second key area of data operations management and involves finding the optimum technology solution for the data management project. The contribution of data operations management to the value of the enterprise's data results from the provisioning of adequate support within the enterprise to ensure that the data assets are maintained, protected, and available.

Metadata Management

Metadata is defined as "data about data" and is used to describe things like data transactions, events, relationships, and other attributes or characteristics about the data. Metadata is vitally important to the valuation of data because it provides context and meaning about the data, including its physical characteristics, the business processes that generated it, data rules, and constraints, as well as logical and physical structures. There are three types of metadata:

1. Business
2. Technical and operations
3. Stewardship

The following is an explanation of each type of metadata, along with some examples for each type.

Business Metadata

Business metadata provides the business users with information that relates the business perspective to its data and includes the following:

- Business data definitions
- Business rules and algorithms that impact the data
- Logical data models
- Regulatory constraints regarding the use of the data
- Data value constraints

Technical and Operational Metadata

Technical and operational metadata provides the technical staff with important information about the data and includes the following:

- Audit controls
- Mappings and transformations from the system origin to the target data stores
- Systems of origin for the data
- Government/regulatory bodies that impact the data
- Business processes that generate, impact, and document the data

Stewardship Metadata

Stewardship metadata provides the leaders of the enterprise with a level of quality assurance resulting from the involvement of the data stewards in the data definition, collection, and storage process. Stewardship metadata includes the following:

- Enterprise data goals and objectives
- Business and technical data definition rules
- Data subject areas, owners, and users
- Data sharing rules and agreements

Metadata Strategy and Architecture

A metadata strategy describes the firm's intent regarding metadata management. Once a metadata strategy is in place, the enterprise should also have a metadata requirements document that sets forth how it intends to fulfill the strategy, including both business and technical user requirements.

Metadata Standards

Metadata standards are important because they facilitate the exchange of data between trading partners and government regulatory agencies. Standards also communicate a higher quality of data as it is processed, analyzed, and exchanged both internally and externally. Some of the metadata standards for *structured* data are the following:

- The Open Management Group standards, including the Common Warehouse Metamodel (CWM) specification, the Information Management Metamodel (IMM), the Open Information Model (OIM), the Extensible Markup Language (XML), the Unified Modeling Language (UML), the Structured Query Language (SQL), and the Extensible Markup Interface (XMI), and The World Wide Web Consortium (W3C) Relational Definition Framework (RDF) for describing and exchanging metadata using the XML.
- The Dublin Core MetaData Initiative has developed a set of interoperable metadata standards for a variety of business and organizational uses—primarily for the online environment.
- The ISO/IEC 11179 standard provides guidance on the formulation and maintenance of data element descriptions and semantic content.

Metadata Repositories

Metadata repositories are a critical component of metadata management because they contain the actual physical data tables in which the metadata is stored. A metadata repository will typically contain a directory of the metadata and a glossary of terms that describe the metadata.

Reference and Master Data Management

Reference data and master data are two very important components within the enterprise data management realm. Here are their definitions:

> *Reference data* is defined as "terms, code values and other unique identifiers, business definitions for each value, and descriptions of the business relationships across the domain data value lists." In other words, reference data is a specialized form of metadata that enables the organization to classify and categorize its data. Reference data is sometimes referred to as the data dictionary.
>
> *Master data* is defined as "data about the business data entities that provide context for business transactions." In other words, master data is the most accurate, definitive data values that exist within the organization about its key business entities. Master data values are considered the "golden asset" within the enterprise, and their existence is highly protected—or should be.
>
> Reference and master data management is *essential* to the creation of data asset value because, together, these two activities provide the authoritative "keys" to the data that is stored within the enterprise.

Data Warehousing and Business Analytics/Business Intelligence Management

Data warehousing is concerned primarily with that part of the data life cycle that involves moving the data from its source(s) to a common enterprise data store. Business analytics/business intelligence management concerns itself with that portion of the data life cycle that extends from the common data store to its presentation and use. The following overview describes both capabilities.

The Data Warehouse

A data warehouse focuses on the storage of data that has been uploaded from a firm's operational systems but may include data from other sources as well. Once the data has been transferred from its sources into the data warehouse, it is ready to be accessed and utilized by end users and other systems. Figure 4.3 depicts the layers of a typical data warehouse.

Business Analytics and Business Intelligence

Business analytics is the "analytical side" of data warehousing and is comprised of tools that enable knowledge workers to monitor, query, analyze, and report on the operational and financial condition of the enterprise. Business analytics and intelligence (BA/BI) generally focuses on three business areas: strategic, tactical, and operational.

Strategic BA/BI is the traditional application of business analytics within the business enterprise for the purpose of determining how well the firm is performing relative to its overall strategy and goals.

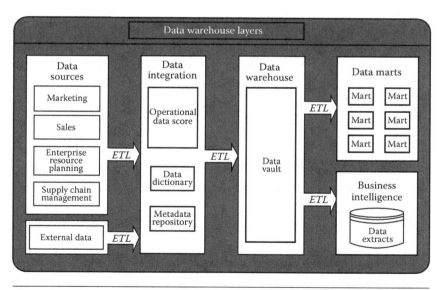

Figure 4.3   Data warehouse layers.

Tactical BA/BI involves the analysis of business trends by comparing metrics from the same periods with the goal of discovering trends that can be exploited for short-term, tactical gain. A robust tactical BA/BI initiative can reveal emerging business opportunities, enabling management to quickly evaluate the marketplace and leapfrog their competitors.

Operational BA/BI provides business managers with insight into the day-to-day operations of the business and often reveals how business activities can be improved or enhanced on a real-time basis.

Data Quality Management

Every enterprise collects data, but not every enterprise collects good data—and figuring out which ones do is key to determining the value of a firm's data assets. In fact, low-quality data can look exactly like high-quality data, so discerning data quality requires a disciplined, methodological approach that examines the underlying processes and systems that generate and store the data.

"Data quality" can be defined as "the expectations held by the owners of data regarding its suitability for a particular purpose." Data quality can vary from repository to repository and from system to system within an enterprise, but a variance in quality does not necessarily make a set of data unusable, nor does all data have to be of the highest quality in order for it to be of value. The important question that must be addressed is "its fitness for use" in a particular situation or context.

The keys to data quality are as follows:

- The business rules that define the data entities used by the enterprise. When applied to data, business rules should describe the origin (i.e., how it is derived), a concise definition, allowable values, and any constraints on the use of the data.
- How well a data entity complies with the applicable business rules.
- A clear understanding within the firm regarding the "acceptability" of a data entity for a particular purpose and also when is it deemed "unacceptable."

Clearly, high-quality data translates into high-value data, making data quality management one of the most important activities under the umbrella of data management.

How Is Data Quality Achieved?

Achieving data quality begins with the creation of awareness within the enterprise that quality is an important goal that will succeed if the enterprise implements a data quality program that includes

- Priorities for data quality throughout the organization
- Standards for data quality throughout the organization
- Relevant metrics for enterprise-wide data quality
- Certification and compliance policies for the organization
- A monitoring and reporting mechanism for data quality

Table 4.2 describes some of the data quality dimensions that an enterprise should incorporate within its data quality program.

Data Security Management

Data security management consists of planning, developing, and executing security policies and procedures designed to authenticate, authorize, access, and track data and information assets. An effective data security management program adds value to enterprise data by engendering trust relationships between trading partners, protecting confidentiality of the data, and providing compliance with government regulations.

The Four Basic Data Security Management Requirements

The four basic requirements of data security management are as follows:

- *Authentication*—validating that users are "who they say they are"
- *Authorization*—identifying the "right" individuals and granting the "right" privileges

Table 4.2   Data Quality Dimensions

DIMENSION	DEFINITION
1. Accuracy	Refers to the extent that the data accurately represents the "real life" entities that it models.
2. Completeness	Refers to the expectation that the data attributes in a database *always* have corresponding values assigned to them and that all appropriate rows are present.
3. Consistency	Refers to the assumption that the data values in one data set are consistent with the data values in another matching data set. This includes the assumption that two data values extracted from two separate, but related, data sets must not conflict with each other.
4. Currency	Refers to the extent to which the data is current with the world that it describes or models. Currency is related to the concept of "freshness" and the up-to-date nature of the data.
5. Precision	Refers to the level of detail associated with the data element, particularly as it pertains to numeric data. For example, truncating and rounding can introduce errors where exact precision is required.
6. Privacy	Refers to the overall ability to control access to data and monitor that access and usage on a continuing basis.
7. Reasonableness	Refers to expectations that the data is relevant within specific operational contexts.
8. Referential Integrity	Refers to the assumption that all data in one column of a table is valid with the data in another column within the same or a different table.
9. Timeliness	Refers to the time lapse between when data is expected to be available and when it actually becomes available.
10. Uniqueness	Refers to the basic assumption that no single data entity exists more than once within a given data set and that a key value exists for each entity and for that entity only.
11. Validity	Refers to the assumption that data values are stored, exchanged, and presented in a manner that is consistent with the domain of values.

Source: "The DAMA Guide to the Data Management Body of Knowledge." (DAMA-DMBOK) 2009 Data Management Association International, Technics Publications, LLC.

- *Access*—enabling the "right" individuals and their "right" privileges to access data
- *Audit*—reviewing the security management program to ensure compliance

Understanding Security Needs and Requirements

In order to understand its security needs and requirements, an enterprise should examine two areas: business requirements and regulatory requirements.

Business requirements are derived from the mission, strategy, goals, and business model. Once the business requirements are documented, the enterprise can identify their data "touch points" which, in turn, usually indicate a security requirement.

Regulatory requirements are derived from various laws and regulations in the global marketplace and virtually every developed nation has a law that impacts data security. Some of the prominent laws and regulations that impact data security are the following:

- Sarbanes-Oxley (SARBOX) and Gramm-Leach-Bliley Act (GLBA)
- Health Insurance Portability and Accountability Act (HIPAA)
- Computer Fraud and Abuse Act of 1986
- Federal Information Security Management Act (FISMA)
- The Canadian Personal Information Protection and Electronic Data Act of 2002
- The CLERP Act of Australia
- The European Union's Basel II Accord
- The European Union's Data Protection Directive of 1998
- The European Union's Data Internet Privacy Law of 2002
- The EU's personal data legislation (2015)

Data Security Policy

Data security management begins with formulating high-level written policies that provide data security governance for the entire enterprise. These policies span both business operations and the IT infrastructure and communicate a coherent security standard to the users, management, and technical staff within the enterprise. Depending upon the needs of the enterprise, the data security policy may include a data classification policy that describes the classifications, levels of control for each classification, and the responsibilities of all users of the data—particularly ownership.

Summary

Like all tangible business assets that are well managed, the data asset is also enhanced when it is subjected to a comprehensive management program. There are nine significant areas of focus within a data management program, which are the following:

1. Data governance—exercising authority and control over the enterprise data assets
2. Data architecture—ensuring that the data is part of an enterprise-wide architecture
3. Data development—creating the enterprise data using industry-accepted methods and tools
4. Data operations—understanding and managing the full data life cycle
5. Metadata management—ensuring that the enterprise data assets have high-quality metadata associated with them
6. Reference/master data management—ensuring that appropriate data is included in the enterprise reference and master data files
7. Data warehouse/business intelligence management—ensuring that enterprise data is stored in a data warehouse and is available for business analytics and business intelligence activities
8. Data quality—subjecting the enterprise data to formal quality control activities
9. Data security—subjecting the enterprise data to formal security policies and procedures

Collectively, these nine areas provide a well-rounded program for adding value to enterprise data assets while also providing metrics for evaluating the value of the data assets within an enterprise.

5

SOME CURRENT THINKING ON THE VALUE OF DATA

Over the past couple of years, several organizations have published research and guidance on the value of data and how to monetize it. These include the MIT Sloan Center for Information Systems Research (CISR), McKinsey Global Institute, *Harvard Business Review*, and Gartner, along with white papers and articles published by KPMG, PwC, Accenture, *CIO Magazine*, and *Forbes Magazine*. The research for this book focused primarily on sources that are generally available to the public, so those organizations that charge fees for their research publications were, for the most part, not included in my review.

As I analyzed the content from the available sources, along with numerous blogs and a patent database search, I uncovered four basic reasons for valuing data. They are

1. Business analytics and business intelligence
2. Leaked and stolen data
3. Data monetization
4. Treatment of data as an asset

This chapter summarizes what I believe are the noteworthy findings and current thinking regarding the valuing of data within each of these four areas.

Let's take a look at each.

Business Analytics and Business Intelligence

Much of the attention that has been given to the value of data is related to business analytics and business intelligence. *Business analytics* refers to the methods, technologies, tools, and disciplines that enable and support data warehousing, enterprise data management, and analytic

45

applications, whereas *business intelligence* refers to "business insights extracted through the use of analytics applied to business data." In other words, business intelligence ideally holds answers to questions such as the following: What is happening in the business? Why has it happened? What do I know about my market, products (or services), customers, competitors, suppliers, and other related business entities? What is likely to happen in the future? What should I do?

Answering these questions—and others—requires both good tools and good data, but how does the data scientist performing the analysis know whether or not theirs is reliable and of high quality? One way to ensure that the data is good is to subject it to a robust valuation process that includes the qualitative metrics needed to verify its overall quality.

Data Leakage and Stolen Data

Data leakage and stolen data can prompt an enterprise to place a value upon their data for a variety of reasons, including the black market value of the data, reputational damage to the firm, financial liability, and competitive implications. Each loss scenario is different based upon the nature of the loss and the type of information that was leaked or stolen. Let's take a look at the two categories of loss and how they occur.

Data Leakage

Data leakage occurs when sensitive or proprietary information leaves the enterprise in an unauthorized manner. There are several ways data leakage can happen, including through

- Cloud storage
- File sharing
- Email
- Social media
- Point-to-point network connections
- Instant messaging
- Dumping files to paper

Most of these leakage scenarios are caused by employees and are not typically motivated by criminal intent. Thus, once a leakage event or situation is discovered, the standard response is to take action to prevent further leakage and then assess the extent and value of the loss. Since information lost through leakage does not actually remove the original copy of the data record, document, email, or other artifact, the value of the loss is generally based upon estimates of reputational harm (e.g., release of customer personal data), damage to competitive advantage (e.g., divulging intellectual property or know-how), and the release of confidential communications (e.g., via corporate email).

Stolen Data

Stolen data occurs when an employee purposefully takes data—which is a form of data leakage with malicious intent—or when an outsider is able to gain unauthorized access to a firm's data and information stores. When a company discovers that some of their data has been stolen, the first question usually raised is "what is the extent and value of the loss?" because the financial liability resulting from stolen data is often far greater than the actual loss of value associated with the stolen data. This is because data thieves usually copy data, rather than actually removing it; thus, the victim retains possession of the data records that were stolen—even though the business value of the data may have been significantly degraded as a result of the illegal act.

Once data has been stolen, the thieves attempt to sell the information on the "dark web" utilizing auction forums, which are largely hidden from the public. The prices for stolen data vary based on the geographical area where the data is being sold, how current it is, and in the case of credit cards, the available credit balance.

Based on surveys by the Ponemon Institute, McAfee Labs, CNBC, and several others, the price of stolen personal data may command the following prices:

- Email addresses and passwords: $0.70–$2.30
- Social Security numbers: $1
- Driver's license scans: $20
- Credit cards without a balance guarantee: $8 per card (number and CVV)
- Credit cards with a $2000 balance guarantee: $20 per card (number and CVV)

- Bank login credentials for a $2000 plus balance bank: $190
- Bank login credentials plus stealth funds transfers to US banks: $500 for a $6000 account balance to $1200 for a $20,000 account balance
- Online payment service login credentials: $20 and $50 for account balances from $400 to $1000; between $200 and $300 for balances from $5000 to $8000

The dark web demand for data extends beyond personal data such as Social Security numbers, credit cards, and banking credentials. Online account information for shopping, entertainment, and social media accounts is also routinely stolen and sold to the highest bidder. Prices for the data associated with access to these accounts range from

- Spotify: $2.75
- Hulu: $2.75
- Netflix: $1–$3

Thomas Holt, a Michigan State University professor who has looked at how data is traded in the illicit market, has concluded that it is difficult to calculate exactly what hackers are getting for stolen data, but a large data transaction can net a hacker millions of dollars.

Data Monetization

Monetizing data as a product or service is a well-recognized business model, and firms such as Dun & Bradstreet, Bloomberg, and State Street Corporation—along with several others—have been very successful with this model. For those firms that do not have a data-oriented business model, packaging and selling data are often a new concept; thus, their definition of data monetization will vary depending upon their business strategy.

According to the MIT Sloan CISR, a survey of nearly 60 executives engaged in data monetization efforts produced an equal number of definitions of data monetization. Among the definitions were "selling data as a new revenue source," "leveraging data to make better decisions," "placing a quantitative value on insights gleaned from data," and "understanding your customers so well that you can proactively make their lives better." These wide variations in the definition of data monetization prompted CISR to develop their own definition, which is as follows:

> The act of exchanging information-based products and services for legal tender or something of perceived equivalent value.

As companies begin to recognize the benefits from business intelligence gained through analytics, executives are embracing the idea that data is an asset, and monetizing the asset offers potentially new revenue streams. This has led many of these executives to ask the question "How can I leverage *my* data assets to generate additional revenue?" As a result, many data monetization initiatives are now underway.

I've organized the discussion regarding monetization of data by the research source, which I think offers a more cogent view of the current thinking. Here are the major sources and a summary of their research findings.

MIT Sloan CISR

Over the past two years (2014–2016), CISR has conducted extensive research on the importance of the corporate data asset and its monetization, resulting in the publication of several papers, presentations, and briefings. The major conclusions gleaned from the CISR research is

- Data is a strategic asset.
- There are six sources of data value.
- Assessing the value of data is important.
- There are three approaches to data monetization.

The following is a brief synopsis of each of the CISR conclusions.

Data Is a Strategic Asset During 2015, CISR surveyed and interviewed data leadership executives from 40 organizations around the globe for the purpose of gaining a better understanding of how their companies treat their data. As a result of these discussions, CISR learned that treating data as a strategic asset means "managing data such that it can be used to create competitive advantage for the firm." In the process of conducting the survey and interviews, CISR also identified three guiding principles that help firms establish and reinforce a view of data as a strategic asset. Those three principles are senior management must clarify data's value proposition; the owner of business outcomes should be charged with data ownership; and the data that matters must be curated. According to CISR, this "clarify-charge-curate" relationship is key to establishing good data management practices and building greater data value over time.

Six Sources of Data Value According to CISR, in order to successfully monetize data companies must draw upon six sources of value. These are

1. Data
2. Data architecture
3. Data science
4. Domain leadership
5. Commitment to client action
6. Process mastery

A brief explanation of these six sources of value follows.

Data To have value, the data must be unique and offer significant value to the marketplace. The value is based upon attributes such as how much is available, how comprehensive it is, how accessible it is, its accuracy and the diversity of sources.

Data Architecture Companies that succeed at monetizing their data often have data support architectures that are innovative and highly customized. These innovations often include software technologies that have been optimized for data management and performance.

Data Science Data science can add value through the discovery of unique relationships within and between database records, resulting in analytics that are superior to the competition. Companies that have dedicated data scientists on staff often invest heavily in relationships with third-party sources of know-how, such as universities, to build their in-house data science expertise.

Domain Leadership Domain expertise is an essential value attribute for a monetization effort. Successful information sellers understand their business domains better than their clients and competitors. These companies hire people who are experts in their domain and industries related to their domain.

Commitment to Client Action   In order to ensure that a data seller's customers are successful and realize business value from the data that they have purchased, sellers offer a variety of value-add services, including customer support, training, toolsets, and follow-up, to measure customer satisfaction and obtain feedback.

Process Mastery   Since data is associated with business processes, those data sellers who master the processes that are associated with their data are in a position to add value to a customer's business by helping them implement business processes that effectively utilize the purchased data and improve competiveness.

Assessing the Value of Data   As a result of research with one of their participating firms, CISR uncovered an approach to data value assessments that they believe other firms can leverage as they seek to perform valuations of their own.

The assessment, which CISR referred to as the Data Value Assessment (DVA), takes an approach using what they call an "upside–downside" analysis. Here's how it works.

First, the firm's leaders assembled a cross-functional team and tasked them with identifying four categories of information technology (IT) projects that involved the use of data. These four categories of projects were basic transaction data, operational data, competitive information, and predictive analysis models. The team then selected representative projects from the four categories and performed bottom-line value assessments of the projects. These assessments resulted in the identification of "lift," in dollar amounts, contributed by each project. For some projects, the "lift" resulting from having completed the project contributed millions of dollars to the firm's bottom line. This represents the "upside" segment of the DVA.

Next, the firm's leaders assembled a cross-functional team comprised of experts from other areas of the firm, including the legal and risk management functions. This team was tasked to perform a "downside" analysis of the corresponding projects assessed by the "upside" team. The downside analysis included looking at things like potential data compromise, cyber risk costs, and internal regulatory costs associated with the individual projects.

Once both the upside and downside analyses were finished, and the upside–downside valuations were tabulated, management was able to have thoughtful, informed discussions about topics such as data governance, data risk, and data classification. These discussions led, in turn, to the creation of a high-level "data-oriented" team tasked with developing new business initiatives that maximized value to the firm while reducing the risks to their stored data.

As a result of their analysis of the DVA approach, the CISR identified five best practices that may help companies overcome the challenges associated with their data valuations. These best practices are as follows:

- Take an enterprise view of data, even if the organization doesn't manage data that way.
- Use cross-functional teams to help ensure that data is evaluated in an enterprise manner.
- Don't perform a DVA just to be doing it; focus value assessments where they really count.
- DVA can potentially elevate management's attention to the importance of their data.
- Keep the data assessment realistic in terms of risk.

CISR believes that the DVA approach is a worthwhile tool for facilitating dialog within the organization regarding data governance and strategies.

Three Approaches to Data Monetization   In summary, the CISR has identified three approaches to data monetization: *selling, bartering,* and *wrapping.* Selling entails exchanging data for money—typically to an aggregator, or reseller, who will generate reports and analytics for resale using the purchased data. Bartering entails exchanging data for another asset—typically an analytical tool or data—that will be used by the bartering firm to improve their products or services. Wrapping entails packaging free data with a seller's information products or services, providing "added value" to customers when they purchase the seller's product or service.

Gartner

Gartner has published several research documents devoted to the topic of data valuation, including a report titled "How Organizations Can Best Monetize Customer Data" and another titled "Why and How to Measure the Value of Your Information Assets." Since these reports are available by purchase only from Gartner, I chose not to analyze them directly. However, several other writers/researchers have referenced Gartner's research on data valuation and I have synthesized their comments. According to these writers and researchers, Gartner asserts that corporate data can be used in two ways to generate monetary value.

Directly Data monetization occurs *directly* when an entity exchanges, sells, or trades data. For example, an individual, who generates data through his/her own efforts or owns a device such as a smart phone, is a "producer of data"—as are business enterprises that do the same. Business entities such as Dun & Bradstreet and Bloomberg that combine data from multiple sources, process the data, and offer it for resale are known as "aggregators of data." Entities—typically business enterprises—that purchase, acquire, or trade data through some trading arrangement are known as "data consumers." Collectively these producers, aggregators, and consumers form the nucleus of the data monetization ecosystem.

Indirectly Data monetization occurs *indirectly* when data is used to create new information-based products or services that leverage the data, although the data itself may not be sold. For example, through the application of business analytics, a retail firm may gain actionable customer insights from their business intelligence, resulting in decisions to provide these insights to their business partners.

Gartner has also coined the term "infonomics" to describe their theory regarding quantification of the value of information and how to manage the asset. Gartner's interest and research investment in the "value of data" area adds significant credence to the topic and its business relevance.

McKinsey Global Institute

The McKinsey & Company's Global Institute recently published a comprehensive study titled "Digital Globalization: The New Era of Global Flows" (March 2016). This 156-page document, which is crammed with statistics, describes in detail the nature of today's digitally connected global economy. According to McKinsey researchers, the concept of "digital flows" is central to the digitally connected economy and data is an integral, if not the most important, element within those digital flows.

The McKinsey Institute researchers point out that back in 1990, the total value of the global flow of goods, services, and finance amounted to $5 trillion. Fast forward to 2014 and the value of the global flow of goods, services, and finance had increased to $30 trillion. This increase in global commerce is about more than just the growth in global trade. It's very much about how global trade has changed. Flows of physical goods and finance were the hallmarks of the twentieth century global economy, but the growth in physical flows have since flattened out, replaced by twenty-first century flows of data and information. Facilitated by the Internet, these changes in global trade underpin virtually all cross-border transactions. The McKinsey Institute researchers assert that, as a result of the digitalization of commerce, globalization has entered a new era defined by data flows that transmit information, ideas, and innovation between buyers and sellers with near-zero marginal costs associated with these interactions.

So, data—in the form of digital flows—is clearly a business asset. The challenge is how to measure the value of these global, cross-border digital data flows. The flow of goods, services, and finance can be measured in traditional terms, such as dollars. However, digital data flows do not lend themselves to the same kind of monetary measurements; thus, a different approach was needed. The McKinsey Institute researchers developed an innovative methodology for calculating the value-added benefits of cross-border data flows and concluded that global data flows have generated as much economic value in the past 10 years as traditional trade networks have generated throughout our planet's entire recorded history.

KPMG

The US-based member of the KPMG network of independent consulting firms has published an expansive paper describing a strategic approach and framework for monetizing data. Titled "Framing a Winning Data Monetization Strategy" (2014), the document offers a framework for considering data sources, a process for the recognition of data value, some business model options, and commercialization alternatives.

The paper begins by declaring that data monetization is not about IT or business intelligence, but rather it "is about effective and timely exploitation of an ever-growing new class of asset, the enterprise data, and converting that asset in currency (profits) by increasing revenues or decreasing costs." The paper goes to considerable length in its argument that data monetization strategy should focus on defining the value of data to the enterprise, its customers, and potential value to third parties.

In terms of "how to" value the corporate data asset, the paper presents parallels between the "data asset" and other categories of corporate assets. For example, a business may use annualized returns to value liquid assets; occupancy rates and maintenance factors to value real estate assets; and material, labor, and indirect costs to value inventory; thus, a business should factor in attributes such as freshness, how it is used, and relationships with other data when attempting to value data. The paper asserts that data is constantly evolving and thus may be appreciating and depreciating in value more or less simultaneously. Therefore, in order for an enterprise to effectively leverage the value of its data, business leaders should recognize the fluidity of data across the enterprise and the embedded value contained in the signals the data may carry as it evolves.

The paper also identifies two categories of data value contributors: performance contributors and predictive contributors. Performance contributors refer to certain key performance indicators that the business has identified and how well the data contributes to the realization of these indicators. Predictive contributors refer to data that have the unique ability to point toward (i.e., signal) certain business outcomes and thus have value based upon their contribution to a better understanding of how business events may turn out.

While clearly marketing oriented, the KPMG paper does contain insightful content about the value of data and how to develop a strategy for monetization.

What Data Is Selling for in the Legitimate Marketplace

Once data has been monetized in the legitimate market, there are a variety of sellers offering an array of data-related products, including the following examples:

- Consumer mailing list: 2.5 cents per record
- Individual criminal histories: $13.95
- Database of US physicians: $239.99
- 4 million fresh email addresses: $75.95 per week
- New York Stock Exchange stock prices feed: $25,000 per month
- Major League Baseball game statistics feed: $1900 per month

If you want to know what your own personal data is worth, *The Financial Times* has published an online calculator that will allow you to determine what your data is likely to be worth as part of a bundle. The figures are based on the analysis of industry pricing data from a range of sources in the United States.

Treatment of Data as an Asset

The fourth reason for valuing data is for the purpose of treating it as a financial asset, much like other tangible and intangible assets are treated on the corporate balance sheet. According to Kim Nash, author of the *CIO Magazine* cover story "CIOs Consider Putting a Price Tag on Data" (June 2014), data possesses inherent value. As evidence, she points to the prices paid for data in the legitimate data market and the importance of accurately valuing a company in a merger or acquisition. Ms. Nash's article referenced several experts who offered reasons for valuing data, including how the data contributes to top-line sales or bottom-line profits, the appropriate level of data protection, its ability to eliminate uncertainty in business decisions, its impact on the firm if stolen, and the benefits of managing the asset well.

The Financial Accounting Standards Board (FASB) apparently agrees. In its Accounting Standards Codification (ASC), FASB has recognized "databases" as an identifiable intangible asset for the purpose of valuing a business in a merger or acquisition. Since the ASC is considered the authoritative source for generally accepted accounting principles, its recognition of "databases" as an intangible asset provides business leaders with justification for treating data as an asset.

Patent Applications Related to Data Valuation

A comprehensive online search of both the US and Espacenet Patent Databases yielded two patent applications related to data valuation. The most relevant application was filed by Robert Schmidt and Jennifer Fisher at Wells Fargo Bank, N.A. The following is a synopsis of their patent application.

Wells Fargo Data Valuation Patent Application　On December 9, 2011, Wells Fargo Bank, N.A. (Robert Schmidt and Jennifer T. Fisher, inventors) filed a patent application with the US Patent Office titled "Valuation of Data" that involves systems and methods for valuing data. In the abstract of their patent application, they assert that their systems and methods can provide a means of determining the initial value of the data asset and calculate a baseline monetary ratio based in part on the initial value of the data. In addition, they claim that their innovation includes being able to measure quality factors, utility, and a new measure of the value of the data asset. In the background section of their patent application, the applicants provide a business case for the valuing of data that I believe is both insightful and informative. The following is a verbatim transcript of their argument for valuing data:

> Data has value, but conventional systems and methods do not value it in the accounting sense. Conventional systems and methods can value many abstract things up to and including goodwill, but do not include a way to value data.
>
> For example, the actual value of a company without its data would be noticeably less than with its data. However, removing a company's data entirely would not change that company's balance sheet, because in conventional systems and methods the data is valued at zero. In actuality, a company minus all the data might be worth only pennies on the dollar. Without the data, value could be lost in a number of ways: there would be no evidence of value, the company might not be able to continue operations, and the cost of reassembling the data could be prohibitive. In some situations, many modern companies (e.g., Internet search

companies or social networking companies) have revenue based entirely on data rather than on physical assets. Thus, in a real economic sense, the data can comprise a large part of a company's value.

Assets that have no value are called "free goods" by economists. Air is a free good, water is a free good. By not assigning any value to data, conventional systems effectively regard it as a free good despite its value. In conventional accounting systems, if a company were to spend an additional 2% of its budget to improve the quality of its data, that decision would only be reflected on the books as if the company spent 2% more money. The improved quality of the data would not be measured or accounted for. Likewise, if a company were to spend an additional 2% to teach users to use the data in its system and help its community get more use of it, to management it would only look like increased support costs, decreased performance, and an increase of 2% in spending.

Thus, although high quality data that is used by more people would seem to be a good thing, any effort to improve the quality and the utility of data is measured in conventional systems as cost with no offsetting gain. The expense is measured, but the increase in the value of the data asset is not. This "data is free" mentality stymies investment in quality data. Because conventional accounting systems and methods do not give data a monetary value, executives and others cannot evaluate efforts to collect, maintain, and improve data in a way that is approachable and easily understandable. Without a measure of the value of data, executives and others lack the necessary information to make the most effective decisions about where investments should be made, for example, whether to invest more on data and less on fuel, etc.

In their patent application summary, the applicants describe their innovation as a system capable of measuring the value of the data asset using a baseline monetary ratio and a nonmonetary measure of quality based on one or more factors. However, it was unclear as to how the system and its methods work in harmony to deliver a valuation of the data asset. Perhaps Wells Fargo will provide a more detailed description of its data valuation patent application at some point in the future.

Thomson Reuters LLC Data Valuation Metric Patent Application   On February 4, 2014, Thomson Reuters LLC (Steven Krull and Michael

G. Thompson, inventors) filed a patent application with the US Patent Office titled "Method and System for Generating a Valuation Metric Based on Growth Data Factors." This patent application addresses methods for analyzing current/historic data to correlate a present/future value for financial instruments utilizing a valuation metric to assess the risk/reward ratio between current stock valuations and current bond valuations. The applicants claim that the invention provides an efficient system and method for determining and distributing a stock/bond valuation, in which the metric accounts for the future growth of the equities. The invention also includes a method and system for (a) establishing the parameters used to determine the valuation metric, (b) calculating the valuation metric, as well as (c) distributing the valuation metric.

The significance of the Thomson Reuters patent application results from the use of the "valuation metric" concept when assessing data. Utilizing a valuation metric can simplify and enhance the overall quality of a data valuation assessment, and do so in a repeatable and predictable manner.

Summary

Clearly, there is a growing interest in the valuing of data—within both the business and thought-leader communities. My research revealed that over the past four years—particularly the past two years—several organizations have begun investigating how to assess and leverage the value inherent in their data assets. I've summarized my research findings regarding the current thinking on valuing data as follows.

At the Macro Level

- Global commerce depends on and is significantly enhanced by digital flows—of which data is the primary component within those flows. Smart companies recognize that those data flows, particularly the "continuous data" flows, associated with business transactions are highly valuable assets. (Source: McKinsey Global Institute)

At the Micro Level

- The business community generally accepts the premise that business analytics/business intelligence can add value to a business, but no published methodology exists to calculate the value of the data used to generate business intelligence. Instead, businesses have focused most of their energy toward monetizing their data assets by offering them for sale and assessing postsale what the data is worth based upon what the market is willing to pay.

  The value of leaked and stolen data is not typically assessed until after an event has occurred, and then the focus tends to be upon assessing the costs associated with the liabilities incurred from the leakage or theft. The dark market price of stolen data varies depending upon the type of data and the extent to which the buyer believes it can be exploited for financial gain. (Source: Multiple sources)

  There is no published formal or de facto method in the public domain for calculating the value of data for the purpose of treating it as a financial asset. (Source: *CIO Magazine* and others)

- Data is a strategic asset, there are multiple sources of data value, and assessing the value of data is important. (Source: MIT Sloan CISR)

- At least one company has attempted to value their data using an internal approach known as a DVA. (Source: MIT Sloan CISR)

- There are three approaches to data monetization: selling, bartering, and wrapping. (Sources: MIT Sloan CISR, Gartner)

- The FASB has recognized "databases" as an identifiable intangible asset for the purpose of a merger or acquisition business valuation. (Source: The ASC, Section 805-2-55)

- The Wells Fargo patent application appears to be an attempt to develop a methodical approach to data valuation; however, exactly how the Wells Fargo method would function remains unclear at this time. (Source: US Patent Database—Wells Fargo Data Valuation Patent Application)
- There is emerging awareness and consensus throughout the business and thought-leader communities that the data within a typical business has inherent value, is in fact an asset, and is as worthy of valuation as the other categories of tangible and intangible assets. (Source: Multiple sources)

6

SOME BUSINESS REASONS TO PERFORM A DATA VALUATION

Knowing what your data is worth can impact your company in many ways. From governance and performance to valuations and security management, valuing your data assets can enhance decision making, improve efficiency, help you grow your business, and increase profitability. This chapter provides an overview of how treating data as an asset can impact each of these areas.

Governance

Valuing data supports improved corporate governance in the following areas:

- Financial statements and reporting
- Data management
- Information technology (IT) projects
- Audit compliance

Here is an overview of each area.

Financial Statements and Reporting

Good business governance begins with transparency in the accounting and financial reporting of the business and its operations. This means that financial statements, such as the balance sheet, should accurately and realistically reflect the value of the different categories of business assets owned by the business.

A balance sheet has three major components: assets, liabilities, and owner's equity. Assets are those things that the company has acquired or produced that have current and future economic value and can be measured and expressed in dollars. Some examples of tangible assets typically reported on the balance sheet are: cash, investments, inventory, property, plant and equipment. Intangible assets are defined as nonphysical assets such as trademarks, patents, copyrights, mineral rights, software, and goodwill.

Figure 6.1 depicts the layout of a typical balance sheet.

When deciding which assets can be included in the balance sheet, accountants are bound by two guidelines: *the cost principle*, which directs the accountant to report the company's assets at their original historic cost, and the *Monetary Unit Assumption*, which directs the accountant to presume that the currency used for valuation will be stable over time. While important to the integrity of the financial report, the combined effect of the cost principle and monetary unit assumption guidelines means that certain valuable resources and assets, such as data, are not reported on the balance sheet.

For example, companies that rely heavily upon data that is generated by and stored within their IT systems are currently constrained from reporting their in-house data assets on their balance sheet because they did not purchase the asset and do not have an accepted accounting method for calculating the cost and value of the asset. When a core asset, such as data, is inadequately or inappropriately accounted for, the omission distorts a company's valuation and can result in an undervalued business.

December 31, 20XX

Assets	Liabilities and owner's equity
Tangible assets	Current liabilities
Current assets	Long-term liabilitites
Investments	
Property, plant, and equipment	Total liabilities
Intangible assets	
Goodwill	Owner's equity
Other assets	
	Total liabilities and owner's equity
Total assets	

Figure 6.1   A typical company balance sheet.

So, how do companies account for their data assets on their balance sheet?

Based on a random survey of Fortune 500 companies, none of them directly reported their data assets on their 2015 balance sheets. This absence of direct reporting of data as an asset does not imply that these companies are ignoring the value of their data. To the contrary, these companies often include the perceived value of the asset within the goodwill category of intangible assets.

For example, on their 2015 balance sheet, Facebook reported $49.41 billion in total assets, of which $18.43 billion was in cash and investments and $18.03 billion was in goodwill. These two assets combined for 74% of the total assets of Facebook in 2015. Given their very public business model, the importance of their customer data, and the extraordinary amount reported in their goodwill account, it appears that Facebook's goodwill account may include some of the value of their extensive data assets.

Indirectly reporting the value of data assets as goodwill on the balance sheet is a standard accounting practice; however, transparency and governance are better served when a firm's balance sheet realistically reflects the value of the data assets and their contribution to the overall financial health of the business. When this happens, senior management is much more likely to govern the business in a way that maximizes the return on their investment—particularly the high-value assets.

Data Management

When a company makes a conscious decision to treat their data as a valued asset, the governance of that asset becomes an important focus across the enterprise. This focus, in turn, can result in the initiation of activities that develop, improve, manage, and protect the data assets of the entire business. In Chapter 4, I referred to these activities as the "Key Data Management Functions." Valuing data assets provides management with the insights needed to make prudent decisions regarding data management initiatives. For example, once a set of data has been assigned a "high asset value," management is better equipped to decide which data management projects are initiated and their priorities.

IT Projects

IT projects typically originate within a firm's business units where business owners conceive ideas for automation or technology-enabled processes. In organizations that have robust IT governance, proposed IT initiatives are subjected to a feasibility study to determine whether the project will fulfill its promised benefits and business value. The result of the feasibility study is the Proposed Project Business Case.

The principle behind the creation of a Proposed Project Business Case is to communicate to senior management the "pros and cons" to be considered before a decision is made to proceed with a proposed project. This focus on business value is important as decision makers try to strike a balance between the costs of pursuing an IT project and the projected business value or expected return on investment. Some of the data-related considerations associated with a proposed IT project are

- Capturing new data entities not previously available
- Knowing how often the data will be accessed and used
- Knowing whether the project adds new value to existing data
- Identifying new risks that might be introduced to highly valuable data
- Understanding how the data risks will be mitigated
- Understanding how the project will impact the existing data management infrastructure

In summary, understanding the value of the data asset provides another set of metrics for consideration when evaluating the merits of a proposed IT project. If senior management is debating the benefits of several proposed IT projects, knowing the value of the data assets that are associated with each project, and how that data value will be leveraged within each project, can help the decision makers arrive at the best overall decision regarding project approval.

Audit Compliance

Annual financial audits are an important tool for business governance, and public companies are required to conduct them annually. Privately held firms with loans and investors are expected to do likewise. A properly performed financial audit will reveal whether the business is properly disclosing its assets and liabilities. Including the value of a firm's business data within the scope of a financial audit will enable senior management, finance and accounting professionals, and other stakeholders to better understand the firm's true market value.

The IT audit is also emerging as an important tool for improving IT governance and many companies have implemented an internal IT audit function to improve IT operations—particularly compliance activities (e.g., Sarbanes-Oxley, Health Insurance Portability and Accountability Act [HIPAA]). Since data is an essential component of a compliance effort, ensuring that it is properly classified and appropriately valued helps the enterprise respond proactively to compliance requirements before an audit is performed.

During an audit, IT auditors are also expected to check the completeness of the firm's IT asset documentation, ensuring that critical assets are documented, ranked, and continuously reviewed as business strategy, policies, and processes change. Business data is an asset, and in order to comply with audit requirements, it should be ranked based upon its importance and criticality to the business.

Performance

Improving business performance is at the top of the priority list for most firms and valuing the firm's data can provide a basis for increasing revenue, improving profitability, and reducing costs. Valuing a firm's data can potentially improve business performance in the following areas:

- Business analytics and business intelligence
- Data monetization
- Reduced operating costs

Here's an overview of each area.

Business Analytics and Business Intelligence

For many firms, "data *is* the business," and having high quality data upon which to base their business analytics is critical! Flawed data will likely result in flawed business intelligence, and flawed intelligence will likely result in bad business decisions. If senior management is contemplating making a significant investment based upon business intelligence gleaned from analytics, the data better be right! Performing a valuation of the firm's data will help identify areas where the data may be flawed or suspect. Data valuation may also reveal potential areas for revenue performance improvement *before* business analytics are applied.

Data Monetization

Businesses that are considering monetizing their data should first acquire an understanding of the overall value of their data. Valuing the data can provide a baseline for determining an appropriate financial return if they choose to market their data and also offer guidance as to which monetization strategy is best—selling, bartering, or wrapping.

A robust data valuation program can also be used as a marketing tool. A firm that has implemented a data valuation program can "promote" the quality attributes that have accrued to their data as a result of having been subjected to a rigorous data valuation process. This will help them differentiate their data product offerings from competing data marketers.

Finally, data monetization offers the opportunity to create an additional revenue stream that can be used to both offset the costs associated with a robust data valuation program and improve overall profitability.

Reduced Operating Costs

Capturing, storing, and managing data assets generate overhead, and in a data-intensive business, these costs can be considerable. Valuing the data assets can provide IT and senior management with insight into which databases, data tables, and data entities represent the highest asset value and liability. These insights, in turn, can be used as a basis for allocating data collection, storage, and management resources toward those data assets that represent the highest value to the organization.

For example, automated supply chains require extensive data inputs throughout the business processes that comprise the chain. Execution of these processes also produces extensive data outputs. However, not all of the data inputs and outputs are necessarily of equal importance in terms of criticality to the operations of the business. A data valuation program will reveal which data is of higher value, and based on this insight, management can make smart decisions about the capture, storage, and management of all of their data—potentially resulting in lower operating costs.

Valuation

Business valuations typically fall into three scenarios or categories:

- Merger or acquisition
- Divestiture
- Private equity investment

Here's how these valuation scenarios might be impacted by valuing a firm's data.

Merger or Acquisition

Mergers and acquisitions are complex business events that typically require a great deal of screening and analysis. The analysis, referred to as "due diligence," may encompass an array of activities depending upon the deal motive and valuation method that is used.

There are two basic perspectives regarding valuation in an M&A transaction: The seller's perspective and the buyer's perspective. Here's how each typically views the role of the business valuation.

Seller's Perspective From a seller's perspective, common motives for selling a business include a desire to "cash out" by the owners or the realization that the potential for survival, growth, and market dominance is much better through a merger or acquisition.

The seller's overall goal is to always enter the deal negotiations with as high a valuation as justifiable for their firm. If the seller is a data-intensive business, it is also in their best interest to perform a rigorous valuation of their data assets in order to ensure that the full value of the asset is reflected in their overall business valuation.

Buyer's Perspective From a buyer's perspective, the two most common motives for pursuing a merger or acquisition are "strategic goals" and "synergies." "Strategic goals" is an all-purpose category of M&A motivators that include the strategic intent to increase or protect market share, access new geographic markets, acquire new products or services, gain access to resources and capabilities, achieve economies of scale, and maximize shareholder value. "Synergies" is the motive when the acquiring firm believes that by integrating the aggregate parts of the target firm with the aggregate parts of the acquiring firm, the resulting business entity will generate benefits that exceed the sum of the separate parts of each firm.

While buyers sometimes pay a premium for a target firm—particularly if there are competing acquirers—it is always in their best interest to acquire at the lowest possible price, so a lower valuation of the target firm is in their best interest when entering into deal negotiations. Since deal motives vary, the valuation method may also vary; thus, the importance of the data asset in the overall valuation process may range from low to high.

Divestiture

A divestiture is defined as "the disposition or sale of an asset by a company." The two most common types of divestitures are "spin-offs" and "carve-outs." Divestitures involve many of the same considerations as mergers and acquisitions, including performing a valuation of the divested business. Here are some data valuation issues that are unique to a divestiture:

- Will any of the data within the divested entity be shared with the divesting entity going-forward, and if so, who will retain ownership of this shared data?
- How will the data that is shared by the divested entity and the divesting entity be divided or partitioned between the two businesses after the divestiture is completed?
- Will the divesting firm relinquish all copies of the data that is associated with the divested entity or will they be allowed to retain copies of all such data files? If they retain copies of the data involved in the divestiture, how will this impact the valuation of the divested entity?

- Will the data management architecture and supporting infrastructure be divested and retained by the divested entity? How will this decision impact the value of the data that goes with the divested entity?

In order to answer these questions, both the seller and buyer need to understand the value of the data associated with the deal and how the asset value could negatively or positively impact the long-term outcome of the transaction.

Private Equity Investments

The private equity industry exists for the purpose of providing investors with alternatives to the traditional equity markets. In order to raise the capital needed for their investment funds, private equity firms must be able to point to a record of success, explain how their record was achieved, and reveal how it will be maintained. Here's a high-level overview of how private equity firms deploy their investment funds.

First they identify a target company based upon their investment strategy, then they perform due diligence, and if their due diligence indicates that the target company is a good investment, they put up some cash and usually borrow the balance needed to close the deal. Typically, a private equity firm will retain ownership and control of an acquisition for about seven years, then either sell the business to another private equity investment firm or take it public through an initial public offering.

One of the keys to building value in a private equity-based investment is to look for the hidden value in the target company and one of those areas is data. By performing a data asset valuation of the target firm during the due diligence phase, private equity valuation analysts can identify potential data monetization opportunities in the target firm, along with potential synergies with other firms in their portfolio.

In summary, a data asset valuation should be part of a private equity firm's investment plan before an acquisition is executed and leveraging the value of the target firm's data should be a component of the firm's strategic management plan after the transaction has been executed.

Security, Liability, and Risk Management

Protecting a firm's information assets is a major concern in today's business environment. Current trading environments, including e-commerce, interactions with customers, and security exposures, necessitate a proactive, vigilant, risk-based posture toward data security. Valuing a firm's data assets can help with data security and risk management in the following three areas:

- Data classification
- Identifying business data liability
- Cyber and privacy liability insurance

First, let's review some of the security challenges related to the data asset, which are

- Availability of data to customers and internal users
- Integrity of the data
- Confidentiality of the data
- Conformity of the data to applicable statutes, regulations and standards
- Privacy and trust protection of an individual's data
- Protection of sensitive data based on organizational requirements

Since it is very difficult, if not impossible, to meet all of these challenges at all times in an affordable, cost-effective manner, a prudent approach balances the security challenges against the risks they pose and their costs. Security risk assessments are used to establish the basis for a balanced data security policy and a detailed inventory of the firm's data is a major input into the security risk assessment. In order to create a detailed data inventory, the data within the business must first be subjected to the data classification process.

Data Classification

According to the Information Systems and Audit and Control Association, the classification criteria used to create a detailed inventory of a firm's data assets are the

- Importance of the data asset
- Data asset owner

- Process for granting access
- Person responsible for approving access rights
- Extent and depth of security controls

The result of the data classification process is some number of data classification categories based upon the sensitivity and criticality of the data to the business. The classification categories can then be used for a variety of purposes, including determining who has access to the data and their level of access.

Subjecting a firm's data assets to a valuation process will aid the data classification process by helping to define the importance of the individual data assets, which in turn will enable the business to perform a security risk assessment and develop a practical data security management plan.

Identifying Business Data Liability

Many businesses have islands and/or silos of data scattered throughout the enterprise—some representing true assets with high value, some with little or no value, and some with a negative value. As a result, some of the data within these businesses would likely appear as a net liability on the balance sheet—if data was included as a reportable asset. There are several reasons why this situation might occur, including

- A lack of seamless integration between application software and associated databases
- Poorly designed databases
- Incomplete databases with missing or obsolete data
- Data created under obsolete applications
- Lack of common data definitions
- Data that has been breached and corrupted
- Data that requires a lot of customization and manual massaging to maintain
- Lack of overall data architecture

Figure 6.2 depicts the functions of a typical manufacturing business, along with the possible interactions and data flows that might need to occur in order for the business to operate smoothly. Collectively, these

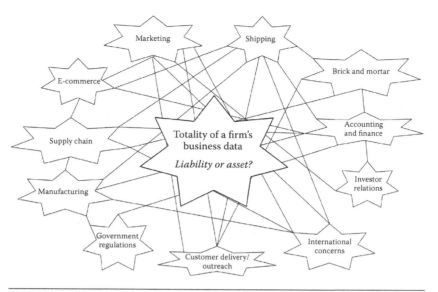

Figure 6.2   Typical business functions and associated data flows.

functions, their associated data and data flows represent some of the potential business liabilities that may exist throughout the enterprise.

Implementing a robust data valuation initiative will uncover much, if not all, of the potential data liabilities that exist within a business by exposing weaknesses in the data architecture, data management, and data security.

Cyber and Privacy Liability Insurance

One of the components of a data security management plan is the risk mitigation plan and one of the emerging tools for mitigating risk is cyber and privacy liability insurance. Commonly referred to as "cyber insurance," this category of insurance is designed to protect a business from claims or losses arising from events that adversely impact the business, its IT infrastructure, and/or assets—including their electronic data. Depending upon the policy, the coverage could include business interruption expenses, remediation costs, data loss expenses, funds transfer loss, cyber extortion, and regulatory fines. So, while cyber insurance may be purchased for a variety of reasons, potential data loss expenses resulting from a breach is the primary reason businesses purchase these policies.

Cost of a Data Breach   There is good reason for businesses to be concerned about the potential expenses resulting from a data breach. According to the Identity Theft Resource Center (ITRC), there were 780 reported breaches in 2015, exposing 177,866,236 records. As of October 25, 2016, the ITRC reported 809 breaches exposing 29,742,941 records. The costs resulting from these breaches are staggering. The Ponemon Institute's *2016 Cost of Data Breach Study: Global Analysis* revealed that the average total cost of a data breach increased from $3.79 million in 2015 to $4 million in 2016 and the average cost paid for each lost or stolen record containing sensitive information increased from $154 in 2015 to $158 in 2016.

Cost of Cyber Insurance   Cyber insurance policy premiums are expensive and policies do not cover all losses resulting from a cyber-related event. For example, cyber insurance policies typically do not cover intellectual property assets or any reputational harm that the insured business may suffer from the event. In addition, policies also have sublimits on coverage payouts. Table 6.1 describes the typical premiums for different liability coverage levels, along with the sublimits of liability for three common costs.

Based on the data in Table 6.1, the annual premium for a mid-sized company seeking $5 million in coverage would be approximately $100,000, with an average annual premium of $20,000 for each $1 million in coverage. Assuming that the $5 million in coverage would likely be reduced through policy sublimits, the actual payout from the policy could be significantly less than its face value, leaving the company to cover the uninsured expenses resulting from a breach.

Cyber Insurance Challenge   Cyber insurance poses a challenge to both potential business customers and to the insurance underwriters.

From the business customer's perspective, protecting digital assets is a top-of-mind issue. The continuing threat of cyber breaches remains high; the cost of the breaches is trending upward, and cyber insurance is a "less than optimal" solution due to its cost and liability limits.

In addition, laws such as the Graham-Leach-Bliley Act, the HIPAA, and the European Data Protection Directive hold businesses liable for customer data breaches, and 46 US states have also enacted legislation that mandates that businesses notify customers of data breaches.

Table 6.1 Cyber Insurance Premiums and Coverage

	TYPICAL PREMIUMS FOR CYBER INSURANCE		
COMPANY SIZE (BASED ON REVENUE)	SMALL COMPANIES (LESS THAN $100 MILLION)	MIDSIZED COMPANIES ($100 MILLION– $1 BILLION)	LARGE COMPANIES (MORE THAN $1 BILLION)
Coverage	$1–5 million	$5–20 million	$15–25 million
Annual premium	$7,000–$15,000 (per million $ of coverage)	$10,000–$30,000 (per million $ of coverage)	$20,000–$50,000 (per million $ of coverage)
	TYPICAL COVERAGE SUBLIMITS OF LIABILITY		
	SUBLIMITS CAN RESTRICT PAYOUTS ON A SINGLE ASPECT OF COVERAGE FROM 10%–50% OF THE TOTAL COVERAGE		
Notification cost	$100,000–$500,000 limit	$500,000–$2M limit	$1.5–$2.5M limit
Crisis management cost	$250,000–$1.25M limit	$1.25–$5M limit	$3.75–$6.25M limit
Legal and regulatory cost	$500,000–$2.5M limit	$2.5–$10M limit	$7.5–$12.5M limit

Source: Deloitte research on insurance provider websites.

From the insurance underwriter's perspective, the cyber insurance market represents business opportunities; however, cyber risks present a challenge as they seek to better understand the nature of the underlying risk.

One of the tools used by underwriters to calculate risk exposure is digital asset inventories; however, many businesses do not maintain up-to-date inventories of their digital assets—particularly their data—thus, they are not in a position to provide the underwriter with this much needed information. As a result, insurance providers often use company size and revenue as a starting point for estimating the premiums.

Given these market challenges, I believe both cyber insurance customers and underwriters would benefit from the adoption of a common data valuation process.

The Data Valuation Stakeholder Community

The community of individuals and groups within the typical enterprise who might be interested in data asset valuations is quite broad. Table 6.2 describes the various categories of stakeholders and their primary reason for being interested.

Table 6.2   Data Valuation Stakeholder Community

DATA VALUATION STAKEHOLDER COMMUNITY	
POTENTIAL STAKEHOLDER	THEIR INTEREST IN DATA VALUATION
BUSINESS MANAGEMENT PROFESSIONALS	
Senior executive/manager	• Protecting, building, and leveraging valued assets throughout the business.
Chief financial officer	• Ensuring that assets are properly valued and reported.
Business unit manager	• Ensuring that valuable data within his/her business unit has an "owner" of record and is properly managed and protected.
Business risk/continuity manager	• Ensuring that valuable data has been identified, that the business risk strategy is consistent with the value of the data assets, and the data assets are protected within the Business Continuity Plan.
ACCOUNTING AND FINANCE PROFESSIONALS	
Certified public accountant	• Remaining abreast of proposed and evolving accounting practices and standards.
Auditor (Accounting)	• Remaining abreast of proposed and evolving accounting practices and standards.
SOME STANDARDS BOARDS AND CERTIFICATION AGENCIES	
Financial Accounting Standards Board	• Remaining abreast of proposed and evolving accounting practices and standards.
International Accounting Standards Board	
Public Accounting Oversight Board	• Remaining abreast of proposed and evolving accounting practices and standards.
American Institute of Certified Accountants	
State Accounting Board(s)	• Remaining abreast of proposed and evolving accounting practices and standards.
International Valuation Standards Council	• Identifying and monitoring emerging valuation standards to ensure that they are properly evaluated before being advocated or promoted as "new standards."
Information Systems Audit and Control Association	• Monitoring emerging and evolving standards that impact the IT audit and security areas to ensure that certification requirements are maintained and up-to-date.
Data Management Association	• Monitoring emerging and evolving standards that impact data management to ensure that certification requirements are maintained and up-to-date.
IT PROFESSIONALS	
Chief information officer	• Ensuring that IT strategy, expenditures, and management have an appropriate focus on valued assets.

(*Continued*)

Table 6.2 (Continued)   Data Valuation Stakeholder Community

DATA VALUATION STAKEHOLDER COMMUNITY	
POTENTIAL STAKEHOLDER	THEIR INTEREST IN DATA VALUATION
Data steward	• Ensuring that high value data is identified, protected, managed, and appropriately leveraged.
Database administrator	• Ensuring that database repositories containing highly valued data assets are administered in a manner that recognizes the importance of the data assets within those repositories.
Database architect	• Ensuring that the overall design of the databases containing highly valued data assets are designed for efficiency and security.
Data scientist	• Ensuring that BA/BI activities leverage the firm's high-value data.
Data security specialist	• Ensuring that highly valued data assets are appropriately classified and protected.
Auditor (IT)	• Ensuring that appropriate controls are in place to protect the integrity and security of highly valued data assets.
BUSINESS VALUATION PROFESSIONALS	
Merger & acquisition advisor	• Understanding how data assets impact business valuation from both the seller's and buyer's perspectives and how to assess data valuation processes to ensure that a data valuation is trustworthy.
Private equity investment advisor	• Understanding how data assets impact business valuation, how to assess data valuation claims/ processes, and how to leverage data value in a private equity investment.
ACADEMIC AND TRAINING PROFESSIONALS	
Accounting and finance	• Remaining abreast of proposed and evolving accounting practices and standards.
Database design	• Staying up-to-date on evolving changes in data standards and how these changes impact database design concepts and principles.
FINANCIAL INSTITUTIONS	
Bank	• Remaining abreast of proposed and evolving accounting practices and standards.
Investor	• Remaining abreast of proposed and evolving accounting practices and standards.
COMMERCIAL SOFTWARE VENDORS	
Database management software	• Ensuring that changes to database management products are designed and implemented in a way that reflects emerging interest in identifying and protecting high value data assets.

(*Continued*)

Table 6.2 (Continued)   Data Valuation Stakeholder Community

DATA VALUATION STAKEHOLDER COMMUNITY	
POTENTIAL STAKEHOLDER	THEIR INTEREST IN DATA VALUATION
Data classification software	• Ensuring that data classification products support classifications based on value.
Data valuation software	• Designing and developing of tools that automate the data valuation process.
BUSINESS AND TECHNOLOGY ANALYSIS, RESEARCH, AND MEDIA PROFESSIONALS	
Business analyst/researcher/writer	• Remaining abreast of emerging thinking and standards in data valuation that could potentially impact business management and stewardship best practices.
Technology analyst/researcher/writer	• Remaining abreast of emerging thinking and standards in data valuation that could potentially impact IT best practices, management, and products.

Summary

Clearly, there are several valid and compelling business reasons for valuing data. These can be summarized as follows.

- Transparency and governance are best served when a firm's balance sheet realistically reflects the value of their data and the asset's contribution to the overall financial health of the business. When this happens, senior management is much more likely to govern the business in a way that maximizes the return on their investment—particularly their high-value data assets.
- When a company makes a conscious decision to treat data as a valued asset, the governance of that asset becomes an important strategic focus across the enterprise. This focus, in turn, can result in the initiation of data management functions and activities that develop, improve, manage, and protect the data assets of the entire enterprise.
- Understanding the value of the data asset provides decision makers with another parameter or metric for consideration when evaluating the merits of a proposed IT project, which can help the decision makers arrive at the best overall decision as to which projects are approved and in what order.

- A properly performed financial audit should reveal whether a business is disclosing its assets and liabilities appropriately and separating data asset value from the goodwill account will result in more accurate and transparent audits, improving governance. IT governance can also be improved by ensuring that all critical IT assets, such as data, are documented, ranked, valued, and continuously reviewed as business strategy, policies, and processes change.
- Subjecting the firm's data to a rigorous data valuing process before it is input into business analytics will result in higher-quality outputs which, in turn, will result in potentially better business intelligence with a higher degree of confidence regarding business insights. Valuing data may also reveal potential areas for revenue performance improvement before business intelligence is applied.
- Businesses that are considering monetizing their data should first acquire an understanding of the value of their data. Valuing their data provides a baseline for determining an appropriate return on their data and guidance as to which monetization strategy is best—selling, bartering, or wrapping.
- Valuing the firm's data assets can potentially reduce operating costs by providing IT and senior management with insights into which databases, data tables, and data entities represent the highest asset value and liability. These insights, in turn, can be used as a basis for reallocating IT resources toward those data assets that represent the highest value and return on investment.
- Valuation of the business is a key consideration in a merger and acquisition, and although the primary parties to the transaction have competing interests, both have an interest in an accurate and transparent accounting of the target firm's assets—including their data. For the seller, this means making sure that the data assets are fully accounted for and included in their valuation, whereas for the buyer, it's making sure that the target firm's data exists, is of high quality, is well managed, and does not pose a significant liability.
- Both the seller and buyer involved in a divestiture need to understand the inherent value of the data associated with the

deal and how this asset's value could negatively or positively impact the long-term outcome of the transaction.

- One of the keys to building value in a private equity-based investment is to look for the hidden value in the target company. One of those areas is the data assets of the target firm. By performing a data asset valuation of the target firm during the due diligence phase, the private equity valuation analysts will be able to identify potential data monetization opportunities that can be exploited post-transaction. The data asset valuation will also reveal opportunities to create growth through synergistic activities between companies within a private equity portfolio.

- Subjecting a firm's data assets to a valuation process will aid the data classification process by helping to define the importance of the individual data assets, which in turn will enable the business to perform a security risk assessment and develop a data security management plan.

- Many businesses have islands and/or silos of data scattered throughout the enterprise—some representing true assets with high value, some with little or no value, and some with a negative value. As a result, some of the data within these businesses would likely appear as a net liability on the balance sheet—if data was included as a reportable asset. A robust data valuation initiative can expose these business data liabilities.

- Cyber insurance is an important tool for mitigating the risks associated with protecting business data. The business customer needs a solid foundation upon which to base their data risk mitigation plan and wants to protect their digital assets in a cost-effective manner, while the underwriter needs to know that a potential business customer has completed a valuation of their data assets, understands the cyber risks, and has implemented a risk mitigation strategy which, in turn, will enable the underwriter to offer a digital assets protection product that is affordable without incurring extraordinary risk and excessive claims. Both parties would benefit from the adoption of a formal data valuation process that includes classifying and inventorying the customer's data assets.

- There are at least nine major stakeholder groups with at least 30 stakeholder roles who have a vested interest in the valuation of enterprise data assets.

Readers of this book will likely discover additional business reasons for valuing the data asset as they contemplate implementing a valuation program.

7

THE OPEN FRAMEWORK FOR DATA VALUATION

The concept of valuing data poses challenges for both enterprises and valuation practitioners. The rules for the treatment of financial and accounting information are governed by numerous regulatory and professional bodies around the world, and any changes to these rules must be carefully examined, debated, and voted on before they are adopted. They are not changed easily or often.

These challenges, along with a host of other considerations, led to the conclusion that the best approach to the development of a data valuation methodology was to invite the stakeholder community to participate in the development of an open framework for valuing the asset.

This approach is known as the "open adoption model."

The Open Adoption Model: A Collaborative Approach

The open adoption model has its roots in the open source software development initiative launched in 1991 by Linus Torvalds. Mr. Torvalds's creation of Linux validated the open adoption model as a practical approach for bringing technology solutions to the marketplace.

The open adoption model is based on the following principles:

- An individual (or group of individuals) develops or creates the initial version of the open source product (or solution) and makes it available to the marketplace as a "free" resource.
- A noncommercial organization assumes the responsibility to solicit input from the community of stakeholders, along with other interested parties, on how to evolve and improve the open source product (or solution) while also providing overall guidance and advocacy.

83

- As the open source product (or solution) is evolved and improved by the stakeholder community, it remains in the public domain and free to all who want to use it.
- Since the open source product (or solution) is not a commercial product, there is no warrant of merchantability or suitability associated with it, and those who use it assume responsibility for any liability arising from its use.

These are the underlying principles supporting The Open Framework for Data Valuation™.

From an Open Adoption Model to an Open Framework

In order for a framework to be considered "open," it should adhere to the following requirements:

- Be comprised of a structure containing building blocks
- Explain how the building blocks fit together
- Provide a set of tools (i.e., methods) for performing the various tasks within the framework
- Provide a common and accepted vocabulary—with definitions where needed
- Accommodate existing standards where applicable
- Be "open"—no patents or copyrights

The Open Framework for Data Valuation was designed to ensure that these requirements for an "open" framework have been met and those requirements will be reinforced as the framework evolves.

Introducing The Open Framework for Data Valuation

The overall structure of the open framework consists of the following building blocks:

- *Definitions*
    Provide a uniform context and consistent vernacular for describing the terms, concepts, principles, methods, practices, etc., applicable to the open framework.
- *Constructs*
    Provide a high-level structure for logically organizing the elements associated with an idea or concept within the

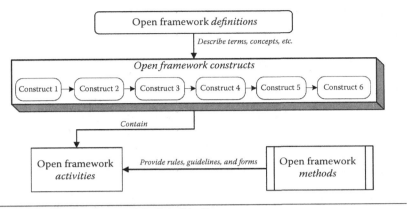

Figure 7.1   The Open Framework for Data Valuation.

open framework. Each construct also contains a stated purpose, description, and outputs.

- *Activities*

    Enumerate and describe the sequential steps required to complete the tasks defined within a particular construct.

- *Methods*

    Provide the rules, guidelines, and forms to follow when performing a step—or set of steps—within the open framework process.

The building blocks are used to create an open framework as depicted in Figure 7.1.

The Open Framework for Data Valuation Key Terms and Definitions

Table 7.1 presents key Open Framework for Data Valuation terms and their definitions.

The Open Framework for Data Valuation Constructs

The Open Framework for Data Valuation consists of six constructs, which are listed in Table 7.2 and depicted graphically in Figure 7.2.

Each of The Open Framework for Data Valuation constructs is explained in the following pages.

Table 7.1 The Open Framework for Data Valuation Terms and Definitions

TERM	DEFINITION
Data	Information, facts, and statistics represented as numbers or text that are collected for reference, observation, measurement, and analysis; that are stored on electronic media; and that are capable of being transmitted in the form of electrical signals.
Structured data	Data that is stored in a consistent electronic form and format that allows it to be prepared for subsequent use (i.e., retrieval, examination, manipulation, and processing).
Data file	Data that is stored in an electronic file typically in a format that can be interpreted.
Database	An organized collection of related data objects, elements, or entities with built-in functional support for updating, manipulating, processing, and retrieving the contents of the database.
Table	A set of rows and columns in a relational database.
Entity	A relational database data object that can be uniquely identified based upon its name and its attributes. Entities can be expressed as nouns, for example, Customer, Employee, and Product.
Attribute	A relational database specification that defines the properties or nature of a data entity. For example, a data entity with the name "Customer" would likely have attributes such as Customer Name, Customer Address, and Customer Gender associated with it.
Data element	A field, column, row, or attribute that describes some data object within a database. It will have a name, a definition, and a meaning. A collection of data elements form a data structure.
Data artifact	A broad term that is used to refer to data in any structured form or format (e.g., databases, tables, entities, attributes, files, records, or elements).
Data unit	A related collection of individual data artifacts that have been aggregated for the purpose of valuation.
Data model	A set of data specifications and related diagrams that reflect the data requirements and designs associated with a particular database. There are two forms of the data model: Logical Model and Physical Model. The Logical Model describes the master data entities, the operational data entities, and transactional data entities and their relationships. The Physical Model is normally embedded within the actual structure of the relational database in the form of database tables and keys.
Transactional data	Data that supports the daily operations of an organization (i.e., captures the business events)
Analytical data	Data that supports decision making, reporting, query, and analysis.

(*Continued*)

Table 7.1 (Continued)   The Open Framework for Data Valuation Terms and Definitions

TERM	DEFINITION
Master data	Data that represents the key business entities upon which transactions are executed, including the terms, code values, and other unique identifiers, business definitions for each value, and descriptions of the business relationships across the domain data value lists.
Reference data	Data about the business data entities that provide context for business transactions.
Fair market value	The price that would be received to sell an asset assuming an orderly transaction between market participants.
Inherent value	The notion that an item can possess value independent of any other item with which it may have a relationship. In other words, it has "stand-alone" value.

Table 7.2   The Open Framework for Data Valuation

CONSTRUCT	DEFINITION
1.	Create and maintain an *inventory* of the firm's data assets.
2.	Identify the *data assets* for potential valuation.
3.	Perform a *Value Metric Analysis* on the data assets.
4.	Aggregate the data assets into *Data Units*.
5.	Select and apply the *Data Valuation Method*.
6.	Create and maintain *Data Valuation Documentation*.

Construct 1: Create and Maintain an Inventory of the Firm's Data Assets

Purpose   The purpose of Construct 1 is to ensure that a complete and definitive inventory of the firm's *structured data* exists and is maintained.

Description   A *Data Inventory* is a comprehensive directory describing the universe of structured data that exists within a firm. Since structured data is, by the open framework definition, primarily stored in database management systems, the source content for the Data Inventory will typically be extracted from the structured databases throughout the firm. The level of granularity in a Data Inventory can vary depending upon the overall goals and philosophy of the firm; the recommended granularity is as follows:

1. Database Name
2. Table Name(s)
3. Entity Name(s)
4. Attribute Name(s)

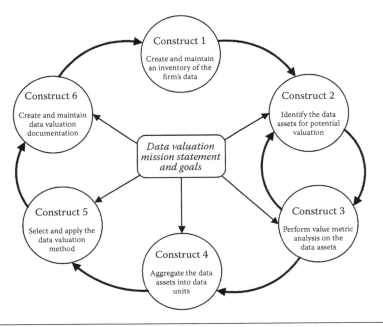

Figure 7.2   The Open Framework for Data Valuation cycle.

There is no prescribed format for the Data Inventory, but it should be organized in a logical format including the three basic categories:

- Transactional data
- Analytical data
- Master data

Additional categories to evaluate include the following:

- Financial data
- Operational data
- Compliance data
- Planning
- R&D

Outputs
- Data inventory

Activities

1. Inventory the enterprise information stores.
2. Segregate the structured data from the unstructured data assets.
3. Create a list of structured data assets for valuation.

Method(s) The following methods may be used to create a Data Inventory:

- Reference Data Management
- Master Data Management
- Data Modeling

Construct 2: Identify the Data Assets for Valuation

Purpose The purpose of Construct 2 is to identify those data assets (i.e., databases, tables, entities, attributes, data files, records, etc.) within the firm that might be considered candidates for a formal data valuation. In effect, Construct 2 provides a preliminary screening for the purpose of identifying the firm's important data.

Description Not all of the data that exists within a typical business has *significant* inherent value; thus, the challenge posed by Construct 2 is to efficiently and correctly identify those data assets that are worthy of being subjected to the formal data valuation described in Construct 3.

The process of identifying the data assets that are worthy of a formal valuation requires a combination of leadership, discipline, professional judgment, and reliable reference materials. First, leadership from senior management is essential to the formation of a panel of internal valuation experts who are familiar with the firm's data and how it is used. Second, an appropriate level of discipline is necessary to ensure that the focus remains on the really important data—as opposed to personal preferences or peripheral data files. Third, professional judgment is needed within the valuation team to understand the implications associated with data structures and data management and how these impact data value. Finally, the firm's *Data Inventory*, along with its *Data Valuation Goals and Philosophy*, is an essential reference source as the valuation team cycles through the data asset identification process.

The data valuation assessment results in an "importance" ranking of high, medium, or low for each data artifact, and the ranking may be assigned to the database, table, entity, or attribute level.

Outputs Ranked list of candidate data assets for valuation (from highest to lowest importance).

Activities The process of identifying data assets for valuation is based upon the following activities:

1. Identify, appoint, and assemble a team of data valuation specialists from within the firm.
2. Perform a data classification of all data assets within the firm.
3. Create data valuation priorities and guidelines based on the firm's valuation goals and philosophy.
4. Perform an assessment of the firm's databases, tables, entities, and attributes based upon importance.
5. Assign levels of importance (high, medium, or low) based upon the data classification.

Method(s) The following methods support the data asset identification process:

- Data Classification (criteria)
- Data Valuation Goals and Philosophy

Construct 3: Perform a Value Metric Analysis on the Data Assets

Purpose The purpose of Construct 3 is to subject the targeted data assets identified in Construct 2 to a set of formal valuation metrics that will result in a "score" that can be used as a basis for financial valuation.

Description   Construct 3 is based upon the following assumptions:

- It is possible to define metrics that accurately and reliably measure the *inherent value* of a data asset.
- It is possible to derive a qualitative score (i.e., raw score) of the inherent value of a data asset.
- It is possible to convert a qualitative score of the inherent value of a data asset into a quantitative score (i.e., weighted score) of the inherent value of a data asset.

These assumptions provide the underlying support for the creation of the *Data Valuation Metrics*, a document that currently defines 12 key categories of data metrics containing 24 submetrics for a total of 36 metrics for measuring the inherent value of business data. These assumptions also provide support for the *Data Valuation Metrics Scoring Method*, an extension of the *Data Valuation Metrics*, which provides the actual method for deriving the "weighted score" of the value of a data asset. Collectively, these metrics are intended to reveal the significance of the data asset to the business, any business liability presented by the data asset, how accessible and easy-to-use the data asset is, and how well the data asset is managed and maintained.

Construct 3 is an iterative process that continues until the data valuation assessment team is satisfied that the valuation scores accurately reflect the business value of each of the assets that were identified in Construct 2. During each iteration of the valuation process, the data valuation team should strive to incrementally improve the precision of their assessments with the overall goal of achieving a reliable and accurate assessment of the value of the data.

Throughout the data valuation and scoring process, the valuation team should remain mindful of the guidelines contained in the firm's *Data Valuation Goals and Philosophy* document.

Outputs
- Metric-Based Data Asset Valuation

Activities   The process of performing a data valuation and scoring entails the following activities:

1. Apply metrics to each data asset that has been identified as being of potential value.
2. Score the results of the data valuation metric analysis.
3. Compile the results in the "Metric-Based Data Asset Valuation"

Method(s)   The following methods support the data valuation and scoring process:

- Data Valuation Metrics
- Data Valuation Metrics Scoring Method
- Data Valuation Goals and Philosophy

Construct 4: Aggregate the Data Assets into Data Units

Purpose   The purpose of Construct 4 is to provide a procedure for aggregating the targeted data assets—*after they have been subjected to value metric analysis*—into groupings that are logically related from a business perspective and share identical metric scores. By aggregating data assets, the total number of entries that may appear on a balance sheet, or other financial report, may be reduced and/or consolidated and the number of valuation calculations is also reduced or combined accordingly.

Description   Large business enterprises may have dozens, if not hundreds, of databases and/or data files that are worthy of valuation and should be included in the firm's financial reports as intangible assets. Simply listing all of these data artifacts could be a monumental task, and the nature of the data assets could be obscured by the sheer number of entries. In addition, data artifacts are often given cryptic names when they are created that do not clearly describe the actual contents of the artifact. Construct 4 has been included in The Open Framework as an optional process that can be used to aggregate large numbers of related data artifacts into data units with descriptive names that are meaningful and simplify communication throughout the valuation process.

Throughout the data unitization process, the valuation team should remain mindful of the guidelines contained in the firm's *Data Valuation Goals and Philosophy* document.

Outputs
- Completed Data Unitization Form (one form for each group of data assets that are to be valued)

Activities The process of performing a data unitization entails the following activities:

1. Assign a name to the proposed Data Unit.
2. Determine the composition of the proposed Data Unit.
3. Populate the *Data Unitization Form* with the names of the selected data artifacts that will be included in the Data Unit.
4. Complete the *Data Unitization Form* and make it available to the data valuation specialist(s).

Method(s) The following methods support the data unitization process:

- Data Unitization Method
- Data Valuation Goals and Philosophy

Construct 5: Select and Apply Data Valuation Method

Purpose The purpose of Construct 5 is to select an appropriate approach or method for the data valuation and then apply the approach or method to the data units that have been targeted for valuation.

Description Once the enterprise has identified the data assets targeted for the valuation process in Construct 2, measured the inherent value of the targeted data using the valuation metrics described in Construct 3, and aggregated the targeted assets into Data Units as described in Construct 4, the next logical step in the overall valuation process is to calculate the *monetary value* of the targeted assets in Construct 5.

Depending upon the enterprise's *Data Valuation Goals and Philosophy*, different methods may be utilized for the monetary valuation. For example, if the goal is to produce a valuation that is acceptable for financial reporting (i.e., balance sheet), then the valuation will likely be calculated using the asset-based fair value approach in accordance with the generally accepted accounting principles that govern that approach. On the other hand, if the goal is to produce a valuation that is acceptable for internal use, and not subject to financial reporting requirements, then a different valuation approach such as the Adjusted Net Asset Method, Adjusted Book Value Method, Market Approach, Income Approach, Cost Approach, etc., may be more appropriate.

Outputs
- Data Asset Valuation Report

Activities The process of selecting and applying a data valuation method entails the following activities:

1. Select Data Valuation Method(s) to be used.
2. Perform valuation calculations.
3. Compile valuation results in the Data Asset Valuation Report.

Method(s) The following approaches or methods may be used depending upon the goal of the data asset valuation:

- Data Valuation Goals and Philosophy
- Fair Value Approach
- Adjusted Net Asset Method
- Adjusted Book Value Method
- Market Approach
- Income Approach
- Cost Approach
- Economic Value-Added Method
- Business Value Index Method
- Enterprise Resource Payback Method
- IT Contribution Model

Construct 6: Create and Maintain Data Valuation Documentation

Purpose The purpose of Construct 6 is to ensure that formal documentation describing the data valuation activities within the enterprise is created and maintained.

Description The Data Asset Valuation Documentation should contain *at least* the following components:

- Data Valuation Goals and Philosophy
- Table of Contents
- Scope of the most recent data valuation and the period covered
- Data Valuation Summary
- Outputs from Constructs 2–5

Outputs
- Data Asset Valuation Report(s)

Activities The process of creating and maintaining data valuation documentation entails the following activities:

1. Assemble all of the forms and collateral materials generated during the data valuation process.
2. Prepare the Table of Contents, Scope, and Summary.
3. Compile the report using the *Data Valuation Report* Template.
4. Preserve definitive electronic copies of all artifacts associated with the data valuation process.

Method(s) The following methods support the data valuation documentation process:

- Data Valuation Report Template

Summary

The Open Framework for Data Valuation was designed with three overall objectives in mind:

- To provide a framework that encourages maximum participation by the community of stakeholders

- To provide a set of building blocks consisting of definitions, constructs, activities, and methods that can be modified as the framework evolves
- To offer enough functional specificity to convince potential participants and stakeholders that it is indeed possible to create a viable framework for valuing the data asset

Hopefully, the framework proposed here will serve as a starting point for a journey that will ultimately result in a comprehensive, accepted standard for valuing the data asset.

8
SUMMARY

The Introduction of this book raised several questions for senior management to consider regarding their business data assets, then went on to assert that the answers to those questions can be uncovered through the application of a data valuation methodology. The assertion that a data valuation methodology would be a useful tool is based on the following premises:

- Data is a business asset.
- Most business data has inherent value, although the level of value may vary.
- Knowing the value of business data enables improved business performance.
- It is possible to value data in a methodical, repeatable, and reliable manner.
- No published methodology currently exists for measuring the inherent value of business data.

Based upon these premises, *Valuing Data: An Open Framework* was developed with the intent of spurring discussion and collaboration among stakeholders with the overall goal of developing a data valuation framework that is acceptable to, and ultimately adopted by, the various stakeholder groups.

The Summary contains a condensed version of the rationale for developing and adopting a framework for valuing business data, presented in a sequential fashion, beginning with Chapter 1.

Chapter 1

Chapter 1 introduces the concept of business data as an asset that is mostly hidden from view as a result of existing accounting rules. It provides a high-level overview of the fair value approach, tangible and intangible assets, and how business data may qualify as both an asset and a liability.

Chapter 2

Chapter 2 offers several perspectives on "what data is," along with some corresponding definitions. These perspectives are analyzed and presented with the objective of identifying a broad data asset category that can be both defined and measured. This analysis resulted in a data asset category called "structured data," which is defined as

> Information, facts, and statistics represented as numbers or text that are collected for reference, observation, measurement, and analysis; are stored in a consistent format on electronic media; and are capable of being accessed, interpreted, and prepared for subsequent use (i.e., retrieval, examination, manipulation, processing, and transmittal).

Structured data is essentially data stored in database management systems and structured data file formats and is the category of data asset upon which the balance of this book and its methodology is based. Obviously, there are other important and potentially valuable categories of digital assets, such as text, voice, video, images, and unstructured data, but the valuation of these asset categories is beyond the scope of this book.

Chapter 3

Chapter 3 provides a recommended approach for determining which data areas to focus on for valuation purposes—and why. Beginning with the contention that business data can be categorized in two ways: Enterprise Data category (i.e., transactional, analytical, and master) and Functional Data category (e.g., finance, operations, compliance, strategic planning, and R&D), the assertion is made that some data is more valuable than other data and how it is used, how often it is used, and its unique contribution to the firm's business goals and objectives should be considered in a valuation initiative.

Chapter 4

Data that is well managed tends to be of higher value than data that has not been subjected to a formal data management program. Chapter 4 introduced nine areas of emphasis typically found within a robust data management program, which are the following:

1. Data Governance—exercising authority and control over the enterprise data assets.
2. Data Architecture—ensuring that the data is part of an enterprise-wide architecture.
3. Data Development—creating the enterprise data using industry-accepted methods and tools.
4. Data Operations—understanding and managing the full data life cycle.
5. Metadata Management—ensuring that enterprise metadata exists.
6. Reference/Master Data Management—ensuring that enterprise reference and master data files exist.
7. Data Warehouse/Business Intelligence Management—ensuring that enterprise data is stored in a data warehouse and is available for business analytics and intelligence activities.
8. Data Quality—subjecting the enterprise data to formal quality control activities.
9. Data Security—subjecting the enterprise data to formal security policies and procedures.

Collectively, these nine areas provide a well-rounded program for adding value to enterprise data assets while also offering a basis for evaluating the value of the data assets within an enterprise.

Chapter 5

There is a growing interest in the valuing of data—within both the business and thought-leader communities, and Chapter 5 presents research findings regarding current thinking on valuing this asset. Those findings include the following:

- Global commerce depends on and is significantly enhanced by digital flows—of which data is the primary component within those flows
- Business analytics/business intelligence can add value to a business, but no published methodology exists to calculate the value of the data used to generate business intelligence
- The value of leaked and stolen data is not typically evaluated until after a loss event has occurred, and then the focus tends to be upon assessing the costs associated with the liabilities incurred from the leakage or theft
- There is no published formal or de facto method in the public domain for calculating the value of data for the purpose of treating it as a financial asset
- Data is a strategic asset, there are multiple sources of value, and the value is important
- There are three approaches to data monetization: selling, bartering, and wrapping
- The Financial Accounting Standards Board has recognized "databases" as an identifiable intangible asset for the purpose of a merger or acquisition business valuation
- The Wells Fargo patent application appears to be an attempt to develop a methodical approach to data valuation; however, exactly how the Wells Fargo method would function remains unclear

There is a growing awareness and consensus that the data within a typical business has inherent value, is in fact an asset, and is as worthy of valuation as the other categories of tangible and intangible assets.

Chapter 6

Given the growing interest in valuing the data asset, several compelling business reasons were identified that justify business data valuations. Chapter 6 presents some of those reasons, which are as follows:

- Transparency and governance is best served when a firm's balance sheet realistically reflects the value of their data and the asset's contribution to the overall financial health of the business.

- When a company makes a conscious decision to treat data as a valued asset, the governance of that asset becomes an important strategic focus across the enterprise.
- Understanding the value of the data asset provides decision makers with another parameter or metric for consideration when evaluating the merits of proposed information technology (IT) projects and expenditures.
- A properly performed financial audit should reveal whether a business is disclosing its assets and liabilities appropriately, and separating data asset value from the goodwill account will result in more accurate and transparent audits, improving governance.
- Subjecting the firm's data to a rigorous data valuing process before it is input into business analytics will result in higher-quality outputs, which, in turn, will result in potentially better business intelligence with a higher degree of confidence regarding business insights.
- Businesses that are considering monetizing their data should first acquire an understanding of the value of their data. Valuing their data provides a baseline for determining an appropriate return on their data and guidance as to which monetization strategy is best—selling, bartering, or wrapping.
- Valuing the firm's data assets can potentially reduce operating costs by providing IT and senior management with insights into which databases, data tables, and data entities represent the highest asset value and liability.
- Valuation of the business is a key consideration in a merger and acquisition, and although the primary parties to the transaction have competing interests, they share a mutual interest in an accurate and transparent accounting of the target firm's assets—including their data.
- Both the seller and buyer involved in a divestiture need to understand the inherent value of the data associated with the deal and how this asset's value could negatively or positively impact the long-term outcome of the transaction.
- One of the keys to building value in a private equity-based investment is to look for the hidden value in the target company. By performing a data asset valuation of the target firm during the due diligence phase, the private equity valuation

analysts will be able to identify potential data monetization opportunities that can be exploited post-transaction.

- Subjecting a firm's data assets to a valuation process will aid the data classification process by helping to define the importance of the individual data assets, which in turn will enable the business to perform a security risk assessment and develop a data security management plan.
- Cyber insurance is an important tool for mitigating the risks associated with protecting business data. The business customer needs a foundation upon which to build a risk mitigation plan that protects digital assets in a cost-effective manner, while the underwriter needs to know that a potential business customer has completed a valuation of their data assets, understands the cyber risks, and has implemented a risk mitigation strategy. Both parties would benefit from the adoption of a formal data valuation process that includes classifying and inventorying the customer's data assets.
- There are at least nine major stakeholder groups, with at least 30 stakeholder roles, that have a vested interest in the valuation of enterprise data assets.

Chapter 7

Chapter 7 introduced The Open Framework for Data Valuation approach, which was designed with three objectives in mind:

- To provide a framework that encourages participation by the stakeholder communities
- To provide a set of building blocks consisting of definitions, constructs, activities, and methods that can be modified as the framework evolves
- To convince potential participants and stakeholders that it is indeed possible to create a useful framework by presenting enough functional specificity to demonstrate its viability

Some Challenges to the Adoption of a Data Valuation Framework...

The process of adopting a data valuation framework and methodology faces significant challenges. First and foremost, the rules for the treatment of accounting information are governed by numerous regulatory and professional bodies, and any changes to these rules must be carefully examined, debated, and voted on before they are adopted. They are not changed easily or often.

As a result, several years may pass before a new method is formally approved and implemented. These delays can hinder efforts to change existing rules and practices—even if a majority of stakeholders agree that changes are needed and would be beneficial. This may cause some advocates to simply abandon their efforts to change things and move on to other pursuits.

Given these challenges, a bifurcated approach to the adoption of a data valuation framework is probably the best path to success.

Taking a bifurcated approach to adoption entails encouraging businesses to implement data valuation initiatives for internal business governance, valuation, and performance purposes, while a second adoption pathway focuses on bringing about changes that may need to be made to current accounting rules and practices. The rationale for taking a "dual-pronged" approach to the adoption process is based on the fact that fair value is the current method for valuing assets for the purpose of financial reporting. In order to establish an acceptable basis for fair value assessments of the data asset, some number of business valuations (e.g., M&A) that treat data as a separate asset must be transacted and made publicly available for reference. So, since the pathway for getting data assets on the balance sheet will most likely require a business valuation history, companies wishing to include data assets on their balance sheet should focus *initially* on implementing data valuations for internal valuation purposes.

Some additional things to keep in mind are the following:

- There are a lot of stakeholder groups, and all of them should have an opportunity to participate in the development and adoption of a framework for data valuation.
- The Open Framework for Data Valuation offers a viable platform for designing, refining, and formalizing an approach to data valuation. Take advantage of it.
- The data valuation framework should remain in the public domain and free of commercial ownership or dominance.

- Think incrementally! Don't try to develop a valuation methodology for all business digital assets in one fell swoop. Start with structured data, then expand and modify the framework as needed to include the valuation of other categories of digital assets.
- Be patient—it will take time to develop and adopt a data valuation standard.

Appendix

Fair Value Approach

The market-based (i.e., "fair value") valuation approach relies on the marketplace to determine what a business asset is worth based upon the assumption that the market will establish a fair price (i.e., fair value) for the asset. The fair value-based approach is defined as "the price that would be received to sell an asset or paid to transfer a liability in an orderly transaction between market participants at the measurement date—assuming that both parties are fully aware of the relevant facts—and neither is under any compulsion to complete the sale."

Based upon the concept of "fair value," the market-based approach is arrived at when two parties take into account the respective advantages and disadvantages that each will gain from the sale of the item or asset and agree to a valuation for the item or asset that is, most often, higher than the valuation that might be obtained in the wider marketplace. For the seller, this means making sure that the assets are fully accounted for, whereas for the buyer, it's making sure that the asset is of high quality and is well managed.

Asset Approach

The asset-based valuation approach views a business as simply a collection of assets and liabilities. The approach is straightforward: Identify the assets and liabilities to include in the valuation, select an acceptable method to measure their value, and the calculated difference between the assets and liabilities equals the value of the business. Based on traditional accounting principles, the asset-based approach is often used when a business has a very low or negative value as a going concern.

The asset-based valuation approach may also be used in conjunction with one of the other valuation approaches, such as the income-based approach, and is a viable approach for valuing information technology (IT) assets such as data, infrastructure, and intellectual property.

Income Approach

The income-based valuation approach focuses on the fundamental reason for running a business—making money. This approach is defined as "estimating a business's future earnings power in order to determine the present value of the business." There are two basic methods for translating a business's expected future income into the present value of the business: The Capitalization Method and the Discounting Method (DCF).

The Capitalization Method is based upon the financial principle that money can be invested in multiple ways at any point in time, and as a result, it has a market value at any point in time. The DCF is similar to the Capitalization Method but works a bit differently. The DCF builds into the value calculation the possibility that the business may fail to generate its current level of net income in the future. Recognizing this possibility, the valuation analyst may use the DCF to calculate the value of the business.

Cost Approach

The Cost Approach is based upon the economic "principle of substitution," which bases the value of a business asset on its cost, rather than the amount, timing, and duration of future economic benefits that may be derived from the asset.

There are two basic methods for arriving at the cost of an asset: *Historical Cost*, which reflects the actual cost that has been incurred to develop the asset; and *Reproduction Cost New*, which reflects the current cost of an *identical* new asset having the nearest equivalent utility to the asset being valued. Of the two methods, Replacement Cost New is generally considered to be the most direct and meaningful cost-based means of estimating the value of an asset. Once the Replacement Cost New for an asset has been determined, various forms of obsolescence must be considered, such as functional, technological, and economic. Physical deterioration is a common form of obsolescence for tangible assets and "out-of-date" is a common form of obsolescence for an intangible asset such as data.

The Open Framework for Data Valuation

Data Valuation Mission Statement and Goals

The Data Valuation Mission Statement and Goals provides decision-makers throughout the enterprise with high-level guidance regarding their data valuation aspirations and activities. It is typically developed as a collaborative effort involving senior management and business unit owners.

Sample Data Valuation Mission Statement

The following is a sample mission statement:

> To treat enterprise data as an asset worthy of being measured, valued, managed, and protected in the same manner as the other assets owned by the enterprise.

Sample Data Valuation Goals

The following are some sample goals:

- To better understand the value of the enterprise data asset
- To efficiently allocate a data management program
- To prepare for a business valuation
- To improve IT governance

- To be able to realistically assess the value of data assets for insurance purposes
- To be able to report the value of the data asset on the corporate balance sheet
- To establish IT project priorities
- To produce high-quality business analytics/business intelligence (BA/BI) results
- To enhance IT audit compliance

The Open Framework for Data Valuation

Data Valuation Metrics

#	DATA VALUE METRIC CATEGORY	METRIC DESCRIPTION AND POSSIBLE VALUE
1.	Data Uses	*Description:* • Refers to the number of applications or systems that use the data. *Possible Value:* The higher the number of applications or systems that use the data – the higher the possible value.
2.	Data Usage Rate	*Description:* Refers to the number of times the data is used in a 24 hour period. *Possible Value:* The higher the number of times the data is used in a 24 hour period – the higher the possible value.
3.	Financial Contribution	*Description:* Refers to the contribution to the firm's financial well-being. *Possible Value:* "Yes" or "No" for each sub-metric
	Revenue	Contributes directly to revenue generation.
	Profitability	Contributes directly to profitability.
4.	Operational Contribution	*Description:* Refers to the contribution to the firm's operational requirements. *Possible Value:* "Yes" or "No" for each sub-metric.
	Transaction Support	Is essential to the processing of business transactions.
	Contractual Support	Is essential to the fulfillment of contractual obligations.
	Supply Chain Support	Is essential to the execution of the firm's supply chain.
	Business Continuity Support	Is essential to the continued daily operation of the business.

	User Satisfaction	Is crucial to delivering satisfaction to both internal and external users.
5.	Compliance Contribution	*Description:* Refers to the contribution to regulatory and/or legal compliance. *Possible Value:* "Yes" or "No" for each sub-metric.
	Regulatory Compliance	Is essential to meeting regulatory requirements.
	Internal Compliance	Is essential to meeting internal compliance requirements.
6.	Intellectual Property Contribution	*Description:* Refers to the contribution by IP-related data to business success. *Possible Value:* "Yes" or "No"
7.	Business Intelligence Contribution	*Description:* Refers to the contribution to the firm's BA/BI activities. *Possible Value:* "Yes" or "No"
8.	Monetization Contribution	*Description:* Refers to the potential to produce revenue through monetization. *Possible Value:* "Yes" or "No"
9.	Liability Contribution	*Description:* Refers to the liability costs incurred if the data is stolen or compromised. *Possible Value:* "Yes" or "No"
10.	Decay Rate	*Description:* Refers to the perceived "shelf life" or "life cycle" of the data. *Possible Value:* "High" or "Low"—where "High" equals a 50% or more decline in value after 12 months without refreshing the attribute(s); and "Low" equals less than 10% decline in value after 12 months without refreshing the attribute(s).
11.	Data Storage Structure	*Description:* Refers to the manner in which the data is stored. *Possible Value:* Select the data file storage structure from the list below that best describes how the data is stored.
	Semi-Structured	Minimal structure. Limited access without additional preprocessing.
	Flat Data File	Delimited data file—requires some pre-processing before access.

Indexed Sequential Data File	Accessible to applications and canned reports.
Highly Structured	Flexible structures with application and ad hoc access.
Hierarchical DB	Complex data structure with some limitations.
Networked DB	Complex data structure with some limitations.
Relational DBMS	Highly flexible data storage with virtually no limitations.
Artificial Intelligence/DB Integration	Advanced data structure with potentially unlimited access.
12. Data Management	*Description:* Refers to the manner in which the data is managed. Possible Value: Select *each* of the following data management practices that are applicable to the data.
Data Governance	Authority and control is exercised over the data.
Data Architecture	The data is part of the enterprise-wide data architecture.
Data Development	The data was created using industry-accepted methods and tools.
Data Operations	The data's life cycle is fully understood and managed.
Meta-Data Management	The data has high-quality metadata associated with it.
Reference/Master Data Management	The data is included in the firm's Reference and Master Data files.
DW and BI	The data is stored in a data warehouse and used for BA/BI activities.
Data Quality	The data has been subjected to formal quality control activities.
Data Security	The data is subjected to formal security policies and procedures.

The Open Framework for Data Valuation

Data Valuation Metrics Scoring Method

The purpose of the Data Valuation Metrics Scoring Method is to provide a tool for assessing the basic business value of a data asset. The method is based upon 12 metric categories that provide a 360-degree view of the data asset from a valuation perspective. The Data Valuation Metrics Table, which appears below the *Data Valuation Form*, contains a list of the metrics, along with their descriptions and possible scores. This method is used in Construct 3.

The steps for applying the Data Valuation Metrics Scoring Method follow.

Steps for Applying the Data Valuation Metrics Method

1. Identify the data asset (e.g., database) to be valued.
2. Enter the name of the data asset on the Data Valuation Form.
3. Perform the data valuation by scoring the data asset using the metrics contained in the Data Metrics Valuation Table. Enter the "Raw Score" on the Data Valuation Form. Repeat this step for each Data Value Metric.
4. Convert the "Raw Score" (i.e., qualitative score) for each metric into a "Weighted Score" (i.e., quantitative score) using the Score Conversion Formula and enter the "Weighted Score" on the Data Valuation Form for each metric.
5. Calculate the asset's overall "Weighted Score" by summing the individual value scores (i.e., the score for each metric) and enter the summary score at the bottom of the Data Valuation Form.

Data Valuation Form

The purpose of the Data Valuation Form is to provide a tool for collecting, tabulating, and summarizing the inherent value of a data asset.

Data Asset Name:					
#	DATA VALUE METRIC	POSSIBLE SCORES	RAW SCORE	RAW-TO-WEIGHTED SCORE CONVERSION	WEIGHTED SCORE
1.	Data Uses	High, Medium, or Low		High = 5, Medium = 3 Low = 1	
2.	Data Usage Rate	High, Medium, or Low		High = 5, Medium = 3 Low = 1	
3.	Financial Contribution				
	Revenue	Yes or No		Yes = 5, No = 0	
	Profitability	Yes or No		Yes = 5, No = 0	
4.	Operational Contribution				
	Transaction Support	Yes or No		Yes = 5, No = 0	
	Contractual Support	Yes or No		Yes = 5, No = 0	

	Supply Chain Support	Yes or No		Yes = 5, No = 0	
	Business Continuity Support	Yes or No		Yes = 5, No = 0	
	User Satisfaction	Yes or No		Yes = 5, No = 0	
5.	Compliance Contribution				
	Regulatory Compliance	Yes or No		Yes = 5, No = 0	
	Internal Compliance	Yes or No		Yes = 5, No = 0	
6.	Intellectual Property Contribution	Yes or No		Yes = 3, No = 0	
7.	Business Intelligence Contribution	Yes or No		Yes = 3, No = 0	
8.	Monetization Contribution	Yes or No		Yes = 3, No = 0	
9.	Liability Contribution	Yes or No		Yes = 4, No = 0	
10.	Decay Rate	High or Low		High = 1, Low = 4	
11.	Data Storage Structure				
	Flat Data File	1		1	
	Indexed-Sequential Data File	2		2	
	Hierarchical DB	3		3	
	Networked DB	3		3	
	Relational DBMS	4		4	
	Artificial Intelligence/ DB Integration	5		5	
12.	Data Management				
	Data Governance	Yes or No		Yes = 5, No = 0	
	Data Architecture	Yes or No		Yes = 5, No = 0	
	Data Development	Yes or No		Yes = 5, No = 0	

	Data Operations	Yes or No		Yes = 3, No = 0	
	Metadata Management	Yes or No		Yes = 5, No = 0	
	Reference/ Master Data Management	Yes or No		Yes = 5, No = 0	
	Data Quality	Yes or No		Yes = 5, No = 0	
	Data Security	Yes or No		Yes = 5, No = 0	
				Total Weighted Score	

The Open Framework for Data Valuation

Data Valuation Form

The purpose of the Data Valuation Form is to provide a tool for collecting, tabulating, and summarizing the inherent value of a particular unit of data.

Data Unit Name:				Date Completed:	
#	DATA VALUE METRIC	POSSIBLE SCORES	RAW SCORE	SCORE CONVERSION FORMULA	WEIGHTED SCORE
1.	Data Uses	High, Medium, or Low		High = 5, Medium = 3 Low = 1	
2.	Data Usage Rate	High, Medium, or Low		High = 5, Medium = 3 Low = 1	
3.	Financial Contribution				
	Revenue	Yes or No		Yes = 5, No = 0	
	Profitability	Yes or No		Yes = 5, No = 0	
4.	Operational Contribution				
	Transaction Support	Yes or No		Yes = 5, No = 0	
	Contractual Support	Yes or No		Yes = 5, No = 0	
	Supply Chain Support	Yes or No		Yes = 5, No = 0	
	Business Continuity Support	Yes or No		Yes = 5, No = 0	
	User Satisfaction	Yes or No		Yes = 5, No = 0	

5.	Compliance Contribution				
	Regulatory Compliance	Yes or No		Yes = 5, No = 0	
	Internal Compliance	Yes or No		Yes = 5, No = 0	
6.	Intellectual Property Contribution	Yes or No		Yes = 3, No = 0	
7.	Business Intelligence Contribution	Yes or No		Yes = 3, No = 0	
8.	Monetization Contribution	Yes or No		Yes = 3, No = 0	
9.	Liability Contribution	Yes or No		Yes = 4, No = 0	
10.	Decay Rate	High or Low		High = 1, Low = 4	
11.	Data Storage Structure				
	Flat Data File	1		1	
	Indexed-Sequential Data File	2		2	
	Hierarchical DB	3		3	
	Networked DB	3		3	
	Relational DBMS	4		4	
	Artificial Intelligence/DB Integration	5		5	
12.	Data Management				
	Data Governance	Yes or No		Yes = 5, No = 0	
	Data Architecture	Yes or No		Yes = 5, No = 0	
	Data Development	Yes or No		Yes = 5, No = 0	
	Data Operations	Yes or No		Yes = 3, No = 0	
	Metadata Management	Yes or No		Yes = 5, No = 0	
	Reference/Master Data Management	Yes or No		Yes = 5, No = 0	
	Data Quality	Yes or No		Yes = 5, No = 0	
	Data Security	Yes or No		Yes = 5, No = 0	
				Total Weighted Score	

Sources

"A Roadmap to Accounting for Business Combinations and Related Topics." Deloitte. December 2009.

Allen, Tom. "Cyber Insurance—An Emerging Market." Aspen. www.aspen.com

Bakker, Alex. "How Do You Put a Value on Data?" *Information Management*. March 1, 2013.

Baldwin, Howard. "Drilling into the Value of Data." *Forbes Magazine*. March 23, 2013.

Barnier, Brian. "How to Improve IT Value Management." *CIO Insight*. February 10, 2011.

"Breach Report Hits Near Record High." Identify Theft Resource Center. January 25, 2016.

Burg, William D., and Singleton, Tommie W. "Assessing the Value of IT: Understanding and Measuring the Link between IT and Strategy." *Information Systems Control Journal*, Volume 3, 2005.

Certified Information Systems Review Manual, 26th Edition. Information Systems Audit and Control Association. 2015.

"CGMA Tools: Three Approaches to Valuing Intangible Assets." American Institute of Certified Public Accountants. 2012.

"CIO Challenge—Measuring IT's Value." *Information Week*. October 2005.

Clendenin, Brian. "Communicate the Business Value of IT." *ITBusiness.ca*. November 2013.

"Continued Attacks to Drive Insurance Market by 2020." *Claims Journal*. July 31, 2015.

"Cyber Insurance: One Element of Risk Management." *Wall Street Journal Risk & Compliance Journal*. March 18, 2015.

"Digital Globalization: The New Era of Global Flows." McKinsey Global Institute. March 2016.

Ennajeh, Leila, and Amami, Mokhtar. "Open Source Software Adoption Model OSSAM." Mediterranean Conference on Information Systems. 2014.

Epstein, Marc J., and Buhovac, Adriana Rejc. "Measuring Performance of IT Investments: Implementing the IT Contribution Model." *Advances in Management Accounting*, Volume 17, Pages 43–79, 2009.

"Fair Value Measurements." *A Summary of FASB Statement No. 157.* Finance and Accounting Standards Board. November 2007.

Feinberg, Donald, Adrian, Merv, Heudecker, Nick, Ronthal, Adam M., and Palanca, Terilyn. "Magic Quadrant for Operational Database Management Systems." Gartner. October 2015.

Floresca, Lauri. "Cyber Insurance 101: The Basics of Cyber Coverage." Woodruff Sawyer & Company. June 2014.

Freidman, Ted, and Smith, Michael. "Measuring the Business Value of Data Quality." Gartner. October 10, 2011.

Guevera, Jamie K., Hall, Linda, and Stegman, Eric. "IT Key Metrics Data 2013: Key Applications Measures: Cost and Staff Profile: Multiyear." Gartner. December 14, 2012.

Haines, Paul, and Wiseman, Mark. "Quantitative Value of Data and Data Management." Noah Consulting LLC. 2013.

Hartwig, Robert P., and Wilson, Claire. "Cyber Risks: The Growing Threat." Insurance Information Institute. June 2014.

Higson, Craig, and Waltho, Dave. "Valuing Information as an Asset." www.eurim.org.uk

"Insurance for Cyber-Related Critical Infrastructure Loss: Key Issues." (Insurance Industry Working Session Readout Report). National Protection and Programs Directorate, U.S. Department of Homeland Security. July 2014.

"International Private Equity and Venture Capital Valuation Guidelines." December 2015. www.privateequityvaluation.com

"IVS 210: Intangible Assets" (Exposure Draft). International Valuation Standards Council. April 7, 2016.

King, Rachael. "The Cost of Cybersecurity Breaches Doubles in the U.K." *Wall Street Journal CIO Journal.* June 2, 2015.

Krull, Steven, and Thompson, Michael G. "Method and System for Generating a Valuation Metric Based on Growth Data Factors" (A patent Application). United States Patent Office. February 4, 2014.

Kuiper, E. J., Gangadharan, G. R., and Janssen, Marijn. "Using IS/IT Valuation Methods in Practice." Proceedings of the Seventeenth Americas Conference on Information Systems. August 4, 2001.

"Learn How to Leverage the Value of Data." Deloitte. 2014.

Masa'deh, Ra'ed (Moh'dTaisir), Tayeh, Mohammad, Al-Jarrah, Idries M., and Tarhini, Ali. "Accounting vs. Market-Based Measures of Firm Performance Related to Information Technology Investments." *International Review of Social Sciences and Humanities*, Volume 9, No. 1, Pages 129–145, 2015.

McGilvray, Danette. "Definitions of Data Categories." Excerpted from *"Executing Data Quality Projects: Ten Steps to Quality Data and Trusted Information™."* Morgan Kaufmann Publishers. 2005.

Mohasseb, Sid. "Framing a Winning Data Monetization Strategy." KPMG. 2014.

Monga, Vipal. "The Big Mystery: What's Big Data Really Worth?" *Wall Street Journal.* October 12, 2014.

Morris, Chuck. "Here's What Your Personal Data Is Going for on the Dark Web." CNBC. July 22, 2016.

Mosley, Mark, Brackett, Michael, Early, Susan, and Henderson, Deborah. *The Data Management Association Guide to the Data Management Body of Knowledge, 1st Edition.* Technics Publications, LLC, Bradley Beach, NJ. 2009.

Nash, Kim. "Putting a Price Tag on Data," *CIO Magazine.* July 2014.

Olakunle, Jide. "Auditing Cyber Insurance Policy." *Information Systems Audit and Control Journal.* Volume 2, 2014.

Pace, Garin, Shapella, Anthony, and Vernaci, Greg. "Achieving Cyber Resilience." AIG, 2014.

Ramanna, Karthik. "Why Fair Value Is the Rule." *Harvard Business Review.* March 2013.

Reilly, Robert. "Intangible Asset Valuation—Cost Approach, Methods, and Procedures" (A Presentation to the Business Valuation Association). September 20, 2012.

Romano, John. "A Working Definition of Digital Assets." *Legal.* September 1, 2011.

Rosenbush, Steve. "Open Source Software Companies Try a New Business Model." *Wall Street Journal CIO Journal.* May 25, 2016.

Schmidt, Robert, and Fisher, Jennifer T. "Valuation of Data" (A patent application). United States Patent Office. December 9, 2011.

"The Data Gold Rush." PwC. 2013.

"The Extra Mile: Risk, Regulatory, and Compliance Data Drive Business Value." PwC Financial Services Institute. April 2015.

"The Art of the Corporate Carve-Out." Sun Capital Partners.

"Valuation of a Business, Business Ownership Interest, Security, or Intangible Asset" (Statement on Standards for Valuation Services). American Institute of Certified Public Accountants. June 2007.

Veysey, Sarah. "Data Scarce for Insurers Covering Cyber Risks." June 10, 2015. www.businessinsurance.com

"What's Your Data Worth?" Accenture. 2013.

White, Andrew. "What Is the Value of Data, Anyway?" Gartner. March 6, 2013.

Wixom, Barbara H. "Cashing in on Your Data." *Research Briefing,* Volume XIV, Number 8, August 2014. MIT Center for Information Systems Research.

Wixom, Barbara H., Buff, Anne, and Tallon, Paul. "Six Sources of Value for Information Businesses." *Research Briefing,* Volume XV, Number 1, January 2015. MIT Center for Information Systems Research.

Wixom, Barbara H., and Markus, M. Lynne. "Data Value Assessment: Recognizing Data as an Asset." *Research Briefing*, Volume XV, Number 3, March 2015. MIT Center for Information Systems Research.

Wixom, Barbara H., and Beath, Cynthia M. "Let's Start Treating Data as a Strategic Asset!" *Research Briefing*, Volume XV, Number 9, September 2015. MIT Center for Information Systems Research.

Wixom, Barbara H., and Ross, Jeanne W. "Profiting from the Data Deluge!" *Research Briefing*, Volume XV, Number 12, December 2015. MIT Center for Information Systems Research.

"*World Economic Outlook*." International Monetary Fund. April 2014.

"2014 AICPA Survey on International Trends in Forensic and Valuation Services." American Institute of Certified Public Accountants. 2015.

"2015 Data Breach Category Summary." Identify Theft Resource Center. December 29, 2015.

"2016 Data Breach Category Summary." Identify Theft Resource Center. October 25, 2016.

"2016 Cost of Data Breach Study: Global Analysis." Ponemon Institute LLC. June 2016.

Index

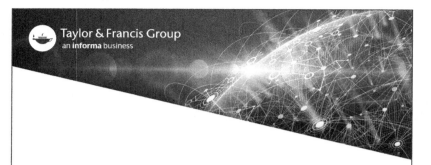